Schooners

Schooners

Basil Greenhill

NAVAL INSTITUTE PRESS

To Mary and C H Ward Jackson

Published and distributed in
the United States of America by
the Naval Institute Press
Annapolis, Maryland 21402

ISBN: 0-87021-960-X
Library of Congress Catalog Card No. 79–91086
Designed by Alan Hamp
Printed in Great Britain
by BAS Printers Limited, Over Wallop, Hampshire

OTHER BOOKS BY BASIL GREENHILL
The Merchant Schooners (2 volumes)
Sailing for a Living
Out of Appledore (with W J Slade)
Boats and Boatmen of Pakistan
Steam and Sail (with Rear Admiral P W Brock)
Westcountry Coasting Ketches (with W J Slade)
A Victorian Maritime Album
The Coastal Trade (with Lionel Willis)
A Quayside Camera
Archaeology of the Boat
Edited and Prefaced: The Last Tall Ships, by George Kåhre
The Life and Death of the Sailing Ship

BY BASIL GREENHILL AND ANN GIFFARD
Westcountrymen in Prince Edward's Isle
The Merchant Sailing Ship: A Photographic History
Travelling by Sea in the Nineteenth Century
Women Under Sail
Victorian & Edwardian Sailing Ships
Victorian & Edwardian Ships and Harbours
Victorian & Edwardian Merchant Steamships

Contents

ACKNOWLEDGMENT

I wish to thank Captain W J Lewis Parker, U.S.C.G. (Retd.) for massive advice and instruction over many years in the study of the history of the large schooners of New England. I am also greatly indebted to Francis E Bowker who sailed in a number of the vessels including the *Helen Barnet Gring* illustrated in this book, and to Captain W J Slade of Bideford, England and Mr Edmund Eglinton of Bleadon without whose help over the years I could not possibly have presented the story of the schooner in this form.

My thanks also go to Ole Crumlin-Pedersen for his help with the Danish material, and to Captain Karl Kåhre for helping with the Finnish material.

LIST OF PLATES

What was a Schooner?

A schooner was a type of sailing vessel. But that is a very much over-simplified statement. She was a sailing vessel, and as far as this book is concerned that means a merchant sailing vessel, a vessel which earned a living for master, crews and investors by carrying cargoes from port to port in return for freight, that is, agreed sums of money, equipped as her main canvas with fore and aft sails, in her case with gaff and boom sails, which, like the principal sails of a modern yacht, could be trimmed only abaft the masts. The gaff sails received the wind on either side according to the direction of the wind relative to the direction in which the vessel was sailing. They were set from masts which were in two parts, a long lower mast and a short, separate (the technical term was 'fidded') topmast. Above the gaff sails, between the gaffs and the topmasts, were set quadrilateral or triangular gaff topsails, also fore and aft.

A schooner had to have two or more masts. If she had only two her main canvas, that is, the biggest gaff and boomsail, could not be set from her foremast. It had to be set from her second or mainmast, or else she was not a schooner but a ketch.

Some schooners, mostly from northern Europe and including nearly all British schooners, set one or more squaresails (see definition in next paragraph) from the fore topmast. These squaresails did not make the vessels anything but schooners, because the two-part masts and the gaff sails as main canvas on every mast were the hallmarks of the schooner, whether she had two, three, four, five or even six masts.

The other great class of merchant sailing vessel in history, much older than the schooner, was the square-rigged ship. Square-rigged ships had at least one mast (and usually two or three) which was in three parts, a short lower mast, a topmast and a topgallant mast, and from each part sails were set from spars slung across the mast and in front of it. These spars were called yards and the sails set from them were called squaresails. They could be trimmed on the foreside of the mast only, so that the wind always acted on the same surface of the sail, the after surface, the back.

The photographs which follow illustrate the definitions given above.

1 This photograph shows a typical square-rigged vessel. She is the wooden barque *Fred* (Peace) built at Bambole Vik in Finström parish in the Åland Islands in the Finnish archipelago in 1920, one of the last two or three classic wooden square-rigged sailing ships to be built in the western world. Her fore and main masts are square-rigged and the structure of the main mast, in three parts, with square sails set from each part, is clearly visible. The mizzen mast, as with all barques, is rigged with a gaff and boom sail and gaff topsail.

As a matter of fact, the only reason the *Fred* was rigged as a square-rigged vessel instead of as a schooner was because the masts, yards, rigging and probably some of the sails of an old Åland barque, the *Per Brahe* which had recently been broken up, were available at the time she was built. It was cheaper to use them than to give her the four-masted schooner rig which would have been the normal thing to do in 1920 and at the time she was built it was expected that she would be converted into a motor ship after she had earned enough money with a year or two of sailing. In fact she was caught by the post-war slump and never made much money and so she remained a barque until her loss in 1933. (National Maritime Museum)

2 And this, above, by way of contrast, is a four-masted schooner rather larger than the *Fred*. Each mast is clearly in two parts. From the lowermasts gaff and boom sails are set. The gaff topsails have been taken in and can be seen bunched at the foot of each topmast except for the gaff topsail on the fourth mast – the jigger – which is still partially set.

This vessel is the *Margaret Thomas*, built at Thomaston, Maine, U.S.A., in 1904. (National Maritime Museum)

3 Compare the four-masted schooner *Margaret Thomas* with the British-built steel four-masted barquentine *Mozart* launched in the same year. Here the foremast can clearly be seen to be square-rigged, in three parts with square sails set from yards slung from each part. The remaining masts are rigged with gaff and boom sails and gaff topsails. Legally in Britain the *Mozart* was a square-rigged ship, since one of her masts was fully square-rigged. This was an important distinction because under the administration of the Merchant Shipping Acts only a master with a square-rig qualification could take charge of her. (National Maritime Museum)

4 We now come to smaller vessels. This is a brig, two-masted and square-rigged on each mast with the addition of a gaff and boom sail set from the main lower mast. She is the *Statsraad Erichsen*, a Norwegian vessel built in 1858 at Horten. (National Maritime Museum)

5 This vessel, to use late nineteenth-century British termi- nology, is a brigantine, with a square-rigged foremast, clearly seen to be in three parts from which square sails, furled in the photograph, are set on yards, slung from each part, and a fore and aft rigged main mast, clearly seen to be in two parts, from which a gaff and boom sail and a gaff topsail, furled in port, will be set when she goes to sea.

This handsome brigantine was a typical product of the shipyards of Prince Edward Island in Canada. She is the *Aquila* and she was launched at Georgetown in the Island in 1888 and she is shown discharging lumber into horse drawn wagons at Newburyport in Massachusetts in about the year 1900. (Peabody Museum of Salem)

6 This photograph when compared with that in Plate 5 shows very clearly the difference between a schooner with square sails on her fore topmast and a brigantine. Both the masts of this vessel are in two parts; both set gaff and boom sails as the main canvas. The square sails are set from the topmast only and the vessel could sail perfectly well, though not so efficiently, without them. She is the *Alice Williams*, built at Llanelly in South Wales in 1854 and wrecked on Skokholm Island, Pembrokeshire, in 1928. She was photographed in Dover Harbour in the early 1920s by Mr Amos, a well known local ship photographer. (National Maritime Museum)

7 Here is a two-masted schooner with no square topsails, sailing entirely on her big gaff and boom sails. Gaff topsails will be set above them when she has got out to sea.

In fact this vessel, the *Elizabeth Drew*, built at Padstow in Cornwall in 1871, was originally equipped with square topsails on her fore topmast but a gaff topsail set on a jackstay from the deck has been substituted for them in order to reduce the crew by one man and save money on maintenance. She also was photographed by Mr Amos off Dover. (National Maritime Museum)

8 This photograph shows another type of two-masted schooner without square topsails. This type of vessel used to be employed in the local trade of the Gulf of Bothnia between Finland and Sweden and is of particular interest in that the big gaff and boom sails were furled by brailing the sails into the masts, like drawing a curtain, rather than by lowering the gaffs to the booms as was done with nearly all the world's schooners, so in these Finnish and Swedish vessels the gaffs were always left aloft. They make interesting illustrative contrast with the big square-rigged ship – a four-masted barque – anchored in the background. The photograph was taken in the West Harbour at Mariehamn in the Åland Islands in the early 1930s. (Ålands Sjöfartsmuseum)

9 This photograph shows a three-masted barquentine. Her foremast is clearly in three parts, square-rigged with yards; her main and mizzen are both in two parts, setting gaff and boom sails and gaff topsails only.

The vessel is a Danish barquentine, the *Hildur*, of Marstal on the Island of Aerø. At the time the photograph was taken she was employed in the logwood trade between the West Indies and Denmark. Some of the big lumber she has brought across the Atlantic can be seen on the quay beneath her bowsprit and jibboom, the long spars which carry the jibs out beyond her bows. (Basil Greenhill Collection)

10 This photograph compared with that in the last plate clearly illustrates the difference between the three-masted schooner with square topsails on her fore topmast and a barquentine. The masts of this vessel can easily be seen to be in two parts – you can see the daylight between the lower mast and the topmast where they overlap. From the fore topmast are set two big squaresails, technically in this case a single topsail and a standing topgallant. In the photograph you can see them furled on their yards. Hundreds of three-masted schooners, particularly American, Canadian and Scandinavian vessels, sailed with an identical rig to this but without the square topsails, and sailed perfectly satisfac- torily. The square topsails, however, although an additional expense in building, maintenance and manning, made the vessel handier, easier to sail and more efficient on long deep water voyages, and easier to put round when on the wind. This vessel is the *Blodwen*, built at Porthmadog in Gwynedd in North Wales in 1891, the first of a series of magnificent small three-masted schooners built at that harbour between 1891 and 1913 which represented the highest development of the wooden schooner in Britain. She is shown anchored off Harbour Grace in Newfoundland where she has gone to load a cargo of stockfish, dried and salted cod. (National Maritime Museum)

How the Schooner Began

The easiest way to present a sail to the wind is square, that is, suspended from a spar to which it is attached at the top edge and which is slung on the fore side of a mast, a yard. Using hand looms it was difficult to manufacture heavy tight woven fabric in pieces of any size. Sails, therefore, were made up of slack woven small pieces joined together. With such material, and with the relatively poor ropes also available, only square sails could be made to set reasonably well (and not very well at that) and so, although it required a lot of gear and manpower to set and handle a big squaresail, squaresails became the order of the day throughout antiquity and through medieval times. When the three masted sailing ship was invented, somewhere in the shadows of the late 1300s and the early 1400s, and very rapidly developed bringing with her an expansion of exploring and seafaring with great implications for the future of western man, she, like the *Fred* in Plate 1, was square-rigged on at least her two principal masts.

Two other ways of setting sails developed in antiquity.

One method was to suspend the head of the sail from a spar, a yard, just like a squaresail, but to sling the yard at the side of the mast and to cant it steeply, so that the head of the sail sloped downwards and forwards. The origins of this kind of sail go back to the Roman Empire and perhaps before. This kind of sail in its earliest known form (nearest the camera) and in a form perhaps even older is illustrated in Plate 11. It was less controllable than the squaresail and needed even more manpower to handle it, but a satisfactory setting could be obtained in this way even with loose, baggy, fabric and such a sail had a better windward performance than the single squaresail. But this kind of sail, later called the lug, the lateen sail or the settee (depending on its shape), because of the huge yard and the great area of fabric in one piece, was not really suited to sailing in big seas and high winds. Apart from the use of long luffed lugs (which probably developed from the square sail in northern Europe) by north European fishing boats with their big crews, it was a sail associated with the Mediterranean, the Iberian Peninsula and the Arab world, but it was used in the north as the lower sail on the third mast of the developing square-rigged ship.

The other way of setting a sail was very simple. This was with the sprit, and was perhaps the most basic of all sail forms. In use as a sail for vessels and working boats in a developed form in the 1st century AD and still in use today in the few areas of the world where the small petrol engine has not taken over completely from sail and oar it is easier to illustrate than to describe and Plate 12 shows spritsails in detail from two aspects.

It will not escape the reader that the boat illustrated in Plate 12 is, in fact, a simple form of schooner, and indeed this was one of the two ways in which the schooner began. A boat like this was simpler to rig and handle than a squaresailed boat, but with the fabrics available, the sails were limited in size.

In fact, to cut a long and highly complex (and as yet incompletely researched) story very short, the schooner in the two forms already illustrated, the schooner with square topsails on her foretopmast and the schooner without square topsails, appears to have developed from two separate sources. One of these was the small two-masted square-rigged vessel which, as advancing technology made the setting of bigger and bigger fore-and-aft sails possible, gradually acquired more and more until they became the main part of her sail area. In this way the schooner with square topsails evolved (Plate 13). The other was the two-mast boat, like that illustrated in Plate 12, which could have gaff sails, with any length of gaff, or triangular sails (leg of mutton, jib-headed, or, as yachtsmen call them, Bermudan) instead of spritsails (Plates 14 and 15). As canvas, ropes and ironwork, got better, so could bigger and bigger sails of these kinds be set on larger and larger boats and vessels. The spritsail, because of the simple way it is supported, grew biggest first and was already large in classical times. From it may have developed the standing gaff with brailing sail, still in use in modern times and illustrated in Plates 8 and 102. From this in its turn may have developed one form of lowering gaff sail, while another may have grown by giving a square head, supported by a stick, to a jib-headed sail. But the origin of the gaff sail is still obscure and it may be much older than the 1600s when it first appears to have become common in northern Europe. From these two-mast boats, or shallops as they were sometimes called, it appears that the schooner without square topsails developed. If this is so, then boats like that in Plate 14 were, several centuries ago, the ancestors of great vessels like the *Margaret Thomas* (Plate 2).

All this is, of course, a great simplification of a very complex development, and one which probably occurred several times over in different parts of the world. There was certainly considerable cross-fertilisation between both types of schooner as the years went on and certainly there were a number of local types with their own evolutionary histories.

The gaff schooner without square topsails began to appear in illustrations very early in the 1600s. Such vessels probably existed therefore in the late 1500s. They were common in the late 1600s both in Britain and in Holland and by the early 1700s both they and schooners with square topsails begin to appear in colonial North America, where the schooner appears rapidly to have become the most favoured rig for a vessel. There were survivors of these early very simple schooners right down to recent years, and there are some even today. Two of these survivors are illustrated in Plates 14 and 15.

There were very good reasons why the schooner of both kinds developed more quickly in North America than in Britain and Europe. Lack of capital to invest in expensive square-rigged vessels, lack of manpower and the fact that schooners required much less work to be done aloft than square-rigged vessels did (work aloft was difficult or impossible in the New England and eastern Canadian winters), probably played their part. Already by the 1760s the illustrations in Des Barres' *Atlantic Neptune* show schooners outnumbering all other types of vessel depicted on the coasts of Maine and Nova Scotia and there are plenty of references to schooners in the diaries of Ashley Bowen of Marblehead which cover the second half of the eighteenth century and a number of drawings of them, the earliest ascribed to 1738. Most of the early schooners illustrated are without square topsails on the foremast, one has a standing gaff and brailing sail on the foremast like the vessels shown in Plate 8.

The development and widespread adoption of the schooner in the United States and British North America was fostered by the Revolution, the Napoleonic Wars and the War of 1812, because by now technology had reached the point at which sailing to windward they were able to outdistance square-rigged pursuers often much larger than themselves. Thus during these long unsettled periods schooners were able to carry the bulk of American cargoes in greater safety than could square-rigged ships.

The developed schooner came back to Britain from North America and the evidence suggests that she came in the late eighteenth and early nineteenth centuries through ports with strong North American trading connections. Perhaps one of the factors in the gradual widespread adoption of the schooner rig for smaller merchant vessels in Britain in the mid-nineteenth century was the development in the first half of the century in Prince Edward Island, Canada, of a great shipbuilding industry, financed largely from Britain and intitially dependent on skilled immigrants from Britain, which specialised in the production of small vessels built for sale on the British market, many of which were rigged as schooners, in due course in the style favoured in Britain with square topsails (Plate 16). These vessels were bought in large numbers by British owners at the ports, Liverpool, Bideford, Plymouth, Bristol, where they were sold. They continued to be built and bought until the 1870s, and in reduced numbers until the end of the century.

The widespread adoption of the schooner (almost always with square topsails) in the merchant shipping industry in Britain in the middle of the nineteenth century and subsequently was at the cost of the small square-rigged vessels, brigs and brigantines, and the big single-masted vessels with gaff sails, later usually referred to as smacks, which had been used in the seventeenth and eighteenth and early nineteenth centuries and all of which were more costly to build, maintain and operate and less handy than schooners. With the widespread adoption of the three-masted schooner rig with square topsails on the foremast after the 1870s the British merchant schooner became a bigger vessel (but still usually not more than 100 feet long) still better able to compete with brigs and small barques in deep sea trade and these latter vessels very rapidly disappeared. At the same time the three-masted schooner was more economical on her gear than the big two-masted schooner and easier to work. From 1870 until the First World War was the great era of the merchant schooner in Britain. The general development of the economy caused her decline and after the war she gave way to the rapid development of road transport.

In North America the history of the schooner took a different course. While small two-masted schooners continued to be built until well into the twentieth century, after the Civil War in the early 1860s the three-masted schooner without square topsails was developed into an efficient, handy, economical and extremely handsome type of vessel, three or four times as big in cargo capacity as her British equivalent and regularly engaged in trans-Ocean as well as long range coastal trades. At the end of the 1870s conditions in the long range trade on the East Coast of the United States made it profitable to develop the four-master, in 1898 (after an initial experiment ten years earlier) the five-master, and two years later the six-master. Although designed as bulk carriers for certain special trades many of these later bigger schooners were taken up from time to time in the general tonnage market and over the years made scores of trans-Ocean passages.

There was a further difference between Britain and North America in the history of the development of the schooner. Whereas the small two-master, always without square topsails on her foretopmast and often with no foretopmast at all, remained the ordinary small schooner in North American waters until well into this century, in Britain a new type of vessel was developed and built in large numbers from the 1870s onwards. This was the ketch (Plate 17), which was in effect a small two-masted schooner without a foretopmast with her masts reversed, so that the smaller mast was aft. the larger, with the gaff topsail, forward. A good ketch was a very efficient, economical and handy vessel costing less to build and maintain than a schooner with square topsails of the same size and needing a man less to handle her.

Although the ketch rig itself was an old one the reasons for its redevelopment in the 1870s are easy to explain. With developing industry and commerce the demand was for larger vessels. The smaller single-masted trading smacks which had been traditional in many British ports and which were too small to have given way to schooners were simply cut in half, the two halves were literally dragged apart with horses, and then they were lengthened by having new sections built into the gap between the halves and the additional smaller mast was added to give them a reasonable sail area. When this process began there was no very strong schooner tradition in Britain and the addition of the small second mast meant that the old mast did not have to be moved.

As the ketch rig proved itself eminently satisfactory for smaller vessels both in the home trade and on deep water there was no incentive in Britain to develop the small schooner without square topsails. But, in the face of the local strong small schooner tradition (and those who have sailed in both have found nothing to choose between the small American-style schooner and the ketch) ketch-rigged merchant vessels were never built and used in North America. So strong did the ketch tradition become in Britain, however, that small schooners and even brigantines were converted into ketches and at least one United States-built two-master (the *Empire* of Bideford, built in 1854) had her masts reversed to make her over into a ketch after she was acquired by British owners.

Ketches and schooners therefore intermingle in the maritime history of Britain, and in that of Denmark and some other European countries. For this reason, despite its title, a few ketches are illustrated in this book.

The schooner rig was the only complete innovation in the history of the sailing ship after the development of the three-masted square-rigged ship in the fifteenth century. The advantages of the schooner over the square-rigged ship were summarised in an article in an American newspaper, *The Bath Independent*, of Bath, Maine, in 1883:

> The schooner is a very economical vessel; she costs less to build, because there are no yards to make and rig. The masts cost less. A smaller crew can handle her with equal safety. Did you ever watch a ship go about from one tack to another? What with rising tacks and sheets and bracing the yards and getting everything snug again, it is a job that is performed when the watch is called so that all hands can have a chance at the sport. Besides that, the ship while in stays often loses her headway and drifts astern part of the time.
>
> But when a schooner is beating to windward, the helm is put down by the man at the wheel. She comes up with her canvas shaking fore and aft. A man shifts the topsail tack and the booms swing over. The mate looks on with his hands in his pockets. Two men only are on deck. She never loses headway for an instant, but gains several lengths every time she tacks. Once around she will run from one to two points nearer the wind than the ship. For the coastwise and gulf trades schooners are unequalled. The most profitable size for the coast trade is one that will carry 800 or 900 tons of coal. For the West India trade larger ones are built, with great success. The whole question of rigging a ship is to get the necessary spread of canvas in the most convenient shape.

The correspondent was writing of the handy four-masters of 750 tons or so which represented the big schooner at its best and he has certainly over-simplified the matter of handling the gaff topsails of a big schooner when putting her round on the wind, but his remarks apply equally to the smaller British vessels and indeed to all schooners. They were handsomely endorsed by an old friend of mine, Captain Ivar Hägerstrand of the Åland Islands of Finland, who commanded the famous steel barques *Loch Linnhe*, *Woodburn*, *Hougomont*, *Winterhude*, *Viking* and *Passat*, and was the last man but one ever to command a laden merchant sailing ship making a rounding of Cape Horn. Between *Viking* and *Passat* for a few months after the end of the Second World War he commanded the Finnish-built West Coast of the United States-style wooden four-masted schooner *Yxpila* (Plate 105) in the Baltic trade and henceforth never ceased to sing the praises of this vessel as one which (especially in comparison with *Viking*) was really a joy to sail.

11 The boat nearest the camera is rigged with a dipping lug sail with a short luff. A sail of identical shape is clearly illustrated on the tombstone of a fisherman who died near Athens in the 1st century AD. It is very likely the classical world also knew a slightly different form of the same sail with an even shorter luff and in consequence a longer and more steeply canted yard. The boat in the background illustrates this type of sail – later called the settee. A third type, with no luff at all, triangular in shape, was and is the lanteen sail.
I took this photograph at Karachi, Pakistan, in May 1953. (Basil Greenhill)

12 This big flat bottomed two-mast boat, with her simple sprit sails, represents, both in hull form and in her masts and sails, a very old north European tradition. She lies today in the German Maritime Museum at Bremerhaven. (Basil Greenhill)

This shews the Schooner Baltick

coming out of St Eustatia y, 16, of Nov, 1765

13 This drawing in the Peabody Museum of Salem in Massachusetts is titled 'This shews the Schooner Baltick coming out of St Eustatia y, 16 of Nov, 1765'. It is now believed possibly to be the work of Ashley Bowen of Marblehead, Massachusetts, who was, among other things, a merchant ship master and a diarist and who served with James Cook in the survey of the St Lawrence which followed the Siege of Quebec in 1759. The *Baltick* was built in 1763 at Newbury, Massachusetts and contemporary customs' records show her to have been employed on a voyage to Guadaloupe from Salem in November 1765. St Eustatius is one of the Lesser Antilles, north of Guadaloupe.

This coloured sketch represents a North American schooner with a square topsail on her foretopmast, a vessel of the type which evolved from the small two-masted square-rigged ship, at a late stage in that evolution. Note that she has both a main staysail like a square-rigged vessel and a gaff foresail like a schooner and that the foremast is in two parts. A number of her contemporaries were bought for British Navy use and represented one of the early channels for the reintroduction of the schooner into Europe.

If Robert Louis Stevenson really meant what he wrote then this, less perhaps the main staysail, is what the *Hispaniola* of *Treasure Island* really looked like, and not remotely like any of the various film ship reconstructions of recent years. (Peabody Museum of Salem)

14 The shallop or two-mast boat, one of the ancestors of the schooner, the forbear of the *Margaret Thomas* (Plate 2) and of the mighty *Wyoming* (Plate 72), widely used in the seventeenth and eighteenth centuries, is still to be found in working use in a few remote places.

I found this one, looking exactly like an eighteenth-century drawing, and photographed her in 1975 at Pointe-au-Loup in the Iles de la Madeleine, an isolated fishing community, part of the Province of Quebec, in the middle of the Gulf of St Lawrence. Shallops of this kind have been widely used in this area for at least three centuries. The loose-footed gaff sails are furled by simply lowering the peaks of the gaffs to the mast, the jaws being left high on the masts in the positions they occupy when the sails are set. (Basil Greenhill)

15 Simple schooners like those used in the eighteenth century on both sides of the Atlantic are still in use in the Gulf of St Lawrence, although all are now fitted with motors. In the autumn of 1978 I saw a few small vessels like the ones illustrated here employed in the local cod fishery on the south coast of the Gaspé Peninsula in the neighbourhood of Anse de Beau Fils. (National Film Board of Canada)

16 This photograph shows a British schooner at the very dawn of the age of photography. It was taken, probably by the Reverend Calvert Jones, an associate of Fox Talbot, in the neighbourhood of Swansea in the early 1840s. The vessel has a number of points of interest; her hull is very sharp, with great rise of floor, much sharper than the hulls of a number of other schooners photographed by Calvert Jones at the same time. The rigging of her foremast, with a single yard with a sail stowed on it, and a top rather like that of a square-rigged vessel in place of the crosstrees of the later schooners, is also interesting. It may well be that she is an early Prince Edward Island-built vessel. (National Maritime Museum)

17 This vessel is the ketch *Progress* built at Kingsbridge in Devon, England, in 1884 for the stockfish trade from Newfoundland. She sailed in this trade for 19 years and once sailed from Newfoundland to the Bristol Channel in 14 days. Like a big American schooner (see the fifth section of this book) she had steel reinforcing straps diagonally across the outside of her frames under the planking, which perhaps contributed to her surviving 62 years of hard work.

When this photograph was taken she was in her old age, with shortened bowsprit and a main topmast little more than half its original length, so that she has a very small main gaff topsail. Her original mainsail would have been at least one cloth broader to take it out to the ends of the boom and gaff and her original mizzen had a longer luff so that the jaws of the gaff would have been much higher on the mast and the whole sail would have been bigger. She also had a big mizzen gaff topsail.

The photograph shows her just getting under way after being anchored at the eastward end of Walton Bay off the Somerset Coast. She is loaded with a light cargo, probably with oats from Ireland destined for Sharpness. The flood is just about to make and the crew are fleeting over the anchor chain on the windlass. In the slack water a puff of wind has driven her up over her anchor cable.

The vessel was fitted with an auxiliary engine in 1918 and it is probable that this photograph was taken in the mid-1920s. Some of her fittings were saved when she was broken up and are on display at the National Maritime Museum's Outpost Gallery at Cotehele Quay in Cornwall. (National Maritime Museum)

The British Merchant Schooners

The British schooner, as I have already said, was almost always equipped with square topsails on her foretopmast, the American had no yards and the small two-masters often had no foretopmast. Though they meant more work in handling the vessel, represented an investment in gear and sails and sometimes meant paying an extra man, the square topsails were considered worth the money. They helped the vessel to go round when sailing on the wind, so that a well-handled British-style schooner hardly ever missed stays, and the squaresails with their great driving power with the wind on or abaft the beam were important on the long deep-water passages made by the British schooners and on the longer passages in the home trade. The short-voyage British vessels, making passages of length comparable with those made by the smaller American and Canadian two-masters without square topsails, were often ketch-rigged.

There is an excellent example of the British approach to the schoooner rig right at the dawn of the use of the schooner in Britain. The *Sultana* was built by Benjamin Hollowell at Boston, Massachusetts, in the early 1760s. Only 50 feet long she was a typical small North American schooner of the period, very like some of the vessels depicted in Ashley Bowen's drawings, with two pole masts without fidded topmasts and, of course, no squaresails. There is a model of her in this state in Gallery 13 of the National Maritime Museum. She made a passage to Britain in 1767 and while there was purchased for the Navy. When she returned to Boston with despatches in November 1768, despite her small size she had been tricked out with fore and main fidded topmasts with yards and square topsails on both.

Very few North American schooners as small as most British vessels made deep water passages in the late nineteenth century. Indeed the development of the use of the schooner rig in Britain, in constrast with its development in the United States and Canada, was confined largely, but not entirely, to relatively small vessels. The rig was rarely used in vessels over about 120 feet long and 200 tons or so gross. There were exceptions, even before the last days of the sailing ship. Big wooden three-masted schooners of nearly 500 tons net and 150 feet long were built in Prince Edward Island, Canada, for British owners and were used in the extremely exacting coal and copper ore trade between Britain and Chile in the early 1870s. In the 1880s and 90s a few steel four-masted schooners of about 1,000 tons gross were built for British owners for use in general deep sea trade, but by then the big merchant sailing ship was already in rapid decline.

During and after the First World War several wooden four-masters, some built on the East Coast and some on the West Coast of North America, were bought by British owners, but none survived the post-war depression. A few steel three-masters of over 200 tons gross were built at Amlwch in Anglesey in the 1890s and they were highly successful in, for instance, the trades to the east coast of South America and in the Baltic timber trade from the Gulf of Bothnia to Britain.

But the typical British schooner was built of wood and was a two-master of up to 80 or 90 feet long, until the 1870s when the three-masted rig became normal for vessels of 80 to 100 feet or so. Her building and ownership usually had nothing to do with the big urban seaports, and she generally did not come from a port on the east coast north of the Thames. She was built in a rural shipyard employing no power or machinery of any kind, at Bideford, Plymouth, Falmouth, Fowey, Padstow, Bridport, Rye, Porthmadog, Amlgwch, Connah's Quay, Ulverston or Millom. Or she was constructed in no yard at all, but at a shipbuilding place where the ground was right to bear the weight of a hull, the slope right for her to be launched into the water and the water deep enough and wide enough to take her away from the slip. In which case she was built by a gang, perhaps of only two or three men, who were got together by a local entrepeneur to build the one vessel, or perhaps one or two vessels, on some bank at some bend in the Truro River, or one of its tributaries, or high up the Tamar, or on the Dyfi, or the Glaslyn or at the back of a beach on the open coast of Cornwall or Wales or Cumbria. She might not have been built in Britain at all, but at a shipbuilding place on a beach of red sand in Prince Edward Island in the Gulf of St Lawrence in Canada, a beach on the shores of a blue creek, edged with dark spruce, and with great blue herons wading in the shallows on the flood of the small tide.

She was owned by shareholders who held between them the 64 shares into which vessel property was divided by the Merchant Shipping Acts. There might be any number of shareholders from one to 64, but usually a dozen or more, and sometimes single shares were held jointly. There was always a legal managing owner who often was the inspiration of the enterprise and who might be a shipbuilder, local mill or timber yard owner, country banker, shipmaster or a broker. Usually the shareholders came from the local community of the sea or river-side village or the small town from which the schooner sailed and they could include the Master, perhaps the mate, farmers, quarry-men, the local

school teacher, the doctor, widows, miners as well as mine captains, ropemakers, shoemakers, sailmakers, coopers, carpenters, builders as well as shipbuilders, lawyers. Prime Minister David Lloyd George's own wife and lawyer brother were holders of shares in Porthmadog schooners in the early years of this century. The risks were well spread, the identification of the vessel with the local community was very close, and there was a strange dichotomy of intense parochialism with an international outlook, with the village schoolmistress and the local grocer, to whom a journey to London was a great adventure, following intently the movements of a schooner in which they held shares between the Rio Grande and Ornskoldsvik.

The typical British schooner was employed in carrying paying cargo between any two ports which had trade which included the movement of consignments of the size she could carry – say from 80 to 250 tons of cargo. She bought Baltic timber from Uleåborg and Sjellefteå on the Gulf of Bothnia to Britain. She carried hides from Rio de Janeiro to France, slate from North Wales to Germany, manure from London to Martinique, phosphates to London from Aruba, granite kerb stones from Sweden to Greenwich, or, equally, likely, from Penryn to the Mediterranean, oats from Ireland to Glouces-ter, slag from Germany to France, copper ore from Huelva in Spain to Devon, coals from Garston to Gibraltar, and coals to Madagascar as well, returning round Cape Horn with cargo from New Zealand. The same vessel in between deep-water voyages carried cargoes from port to port around the coasts of Britain.

Many small schooners hardly ever went on deep water but spent most of their lives carrying cargoes from port to port around the coasts of the United Kingdom and to the continental ports within the limits of the home trade, that is, between Brest and the Elbe, the area of responsibility of the Home Fleet in the Napoleonic Wars which became enshrined in the Merchant Shipping Acts as the area to which a vessel of a certain size could trade without the complications and expense of having to have a certificated master in charge of her. The home trade was a very arduous business requiring the continuous application of very great skill in seamanship. It was quite a different life from deep-water, long voyage, sailing, and in many ways more challenging.

Perhaps, if she came from the south west or the south coast the schooner might carry ripening oranges from the Azores to London or Bristol, that is, before compound engined steamships were developed in the 1860s and an artificial harbour built at Ponta Delgada so that the steamships could quickly load the oranges. This was an élite trade, a luxury trade, one in which high speeds and regular passages were required of vessels which competed for regular fixtures in the business. It gave rise to fast vessels with awkward hull shapes and relatively small cargo capacity which were not really suitable for many other trades. But the influence of these vessels – and some of the schooners themselves – lingered on, especially in the west country.

But whatever else she did, the chances are that any British schooner except those confined entirely to the home trade at some stage in her career carried salt to Newfoundland or Labrador from the Mediterranean or the Iberian Peninsula and returned to Europe, north or south, with dried and salted cod fish in bulk. For the Newfoundland trade was at the heart of the British schooner's world particularly in the later nineteenth century when the schooners were at their height in numbers and the tonnage of cargo they carried. By its very essence this was a small-ship trade. The cod was caught either from boats based on the small harbours and creeks of the Newfoundland and Labrador coasts or from schooners, some of them dory carriers, which lay out on the distant banks for weeks on end or nearer the shores of Newfoundland for a shorter period. But most of it was caught from home-based boats.

As soon as possible after they were caught the fish were beheaded, boned and cleaned, and then washed and salted. There were various ways of drying and salting the fish, afloat or ashore, but most of the Newfoundland fish caught in the inshore fishery were dried by the fishermen and their women in the small settlements to which they belonged. The fish drying stages, called 'flakes', can still be seen at a few places in Newfoundland and on the Gaspé Peninsula in Quebec. The fish caught on the Labrador, where the weather was usually not suitable for drying, were salted and then either taken in salt bulk to the Newfoundland settlements or direct to Europe in the British schooners. Much of the work of preparing the fish ashore in Labrador was done by women from Newfoundland who came in their scores by schooner from the Newfoundland outposts for each season's work.

The results of all these processes of fishing were the same. Small packets making up in total large quantities of the finished product lay awaiting collection at all the obscure and inaccessible settlements of the shattered coasts of Newfoundland while bulk salted cargoes were gathered in the creeks of the Labrador, both countries very deficient in land transport. The collection of these cargoes was both physically and economically a small-vessel trade for which schooners with their low costs and low overheads were particularly suitable.

It had been in existence since the 1400s, and salt fish had been an important item in European diet since late medieval times, indeed the salt cod industry has constituted for centuries an important economic and political factor in the history of the nations engaged in it. After the development of the schooner, and particularly after the widespread adoption of the three-master in Britain at the beginning of the 1870s, the business, then at its greatest, became a schooner trade and the farmer and the widow in Fowey or Salcombe or Bideford or Porthmadog added to the strangely named ports with which they were familiar; such places as Harbour Buffett, Carbonear, Renews, Battle Harbour, Venison Tickle, Tilt Cove, Peggy's Bag, Joe Batts Arm, and Brigus. In these little harbours and cracks in the rock, Newfoundland outports and Labrador fishing places, the British schooners loaded for Genoa, Lisbon, Valencia, Gibraltar, Zanté, Plymouth, Exeter, Poole, Bristol, Naples and Leghorn.

These vessels of under 200 tons, many of them below 100, so that under the Merchant Shipping Acts they did not have to carry a certificated mate, kept to the hard North Atlantic trade year in and year out. To give a few examples, the *Blodwen* of Porthmadog (Plate 10) probably did not miss a single season in Newfoundland throughout her life of 25 years. The little two-master *Cadwalader Jones* was in the Newfoundland trade for 38 years. The ketch *Progress* (Plate 17) sailed to Newfoundland twice a year every year for 19 years. The two-masted schooners from Fowey managed by John Stephens and his family, *Little Secret, Little Wonder, Little Mystery, Little Gem*, and others, specialised in the Newfoundland business and many of them were employed in it almost exclusively when not carrying cargoes between home ports. John Stephens owned the fastest of all the small schooners, the *Isabella*, which in 1900 sailed from Fowey to Spain, eight times across the Atlantic and back to Fowey from Spain in seven months and 22 days. She was 75 feet long and had a crew of four.

It was in the Newfoundland trade that the British schooner was developed to its finest form in the shipyards of Porthmadog in the County of Gwynedd in North Wales. This development occurred between 1891 when the *Blodwen* (Plate 10) was launched and 1913 when the last of the Porthmadog schooners was built. The vessels built over these years were three-masted schooners of very similar size and hull shape, a conscious attempt by Porthmadog shipbuilders and owners to design and produce an ideal small merchant sailing ship to trade continuously under all conditions on deep water. These vessels, known locally as the 'Western Ocean Yachts' were highly successful in the North Atlantic trade and equally profitable in the home trade.

The Newfoundland trade persisted until the Second World War but by then it was in the hands of Danish and Nova Scotian schooners. As late as 1939 I watched a Danish schooner, the *Start* of Marstal, set sail from Bristol towards Indian Tickle in Labrador to load fish. The last British vessel to sail in this historic business was the *Lady St Johns*, built at Kingsbridge in Devon, and when she made her last trans-Atlantic passage under British ownership in 1930 she was the last British merchant sailing vessel in a sailing vessel trade which had continued uninterrupted for four and a half centuries.

In 1890 British merchant sailing vessels registered as of ports in the United Kingdom totalled just under three million tons net. In the same year some 171,000 tons of shipping was listed in Lloyd's Register as schooner or ketch-rigged and registered at a home port in the United Kingdom. It would be a conservative estimate to add 50% to the Lloyd's total to include vessels registered under the Merchant Shipping Acts but not listed by Lloyds. The total tonnage of schooners from United Kingdom ports therefore was very roughly some $7\frac{1}{2}\%$ of all sailing vessel tonnage registered at United Kingdom home ports in 1890.

For a complex of reasons the British schooner survived long after big square-rigged sailing ships had ceased to sail for British owners. The small steamer, because of her high overheads and the fact that she could not be built shallow enough to use many tidal berths to load and discharge, could not offer serious competition to the schooners working between small ports in the home trade and as long as there were small consignments of cargo to be carried on deep water at rates quite uneconomic for steam vessels the schooner continued in trade. It was less the powered vessel than the general development of industry, the size of cargoes, and the development of road transport which finished the merchant schooners in Britain. Although none was built

after the outbreak of the First World War they continued in use, both in deep water and in the home trade, until the end of the 1920s. Many continued to work around the coasts until the Second World War. A very few, equipped with powerful diesel engines and run as motor ships, survived even longer. So it is true to say that the merchant schooner in Britain, albeit in the form of a vessel using sails to back up her diesel, did survive into the space age.

18 This photograph shows a classic fruit schooner, the *Queen of the West* in her old age lying at anchor off Liverpool. She was built at Salcombe in Devon in 1849 and employed in the trade to Britain with ripening oranges from the Azores. The sheer is flat. Unlike the big American schooners and the wooden barques a vessel of this size will not have hogged – sagged at the ends – much, even in 75 years of active life. An early painting shows that the *Queen of the West* was, like many of her contemporaries, very flat-sheered even when she was new. The curved, raking, stem and the sharp waterlines forward (which made her very wet in a sea) are all characteristic of the fruit schooners, which were built to get their small, light, cargoes home to Britain as quickly as possible. When she was in the fruit trade she carried an extra yard and squaresail, but otherwise was rigged much as she is seen in this photograph taken in the 1920s. (Basil Greenhill Collection)

19 The *Susan Vittery*, shown here at Falmouth loading china clay, was built as a two-masted schooner at Dartmouth, Devon, in 1859, the shareholders including members of the Vittery family of Brixham. She spent years in the Azores orange trade and other deep water trades and was subsequently employed principally in the Newfoundland trade. This photograph was taken after 1903 when she was rerigged as a more handy and economical three-masted schooner, a change which meant less wear and tear on her gear, and probably a man less in the crew.

There are a number of odd things to be seen in this photograph. The vessel has no boom, gaff, or sails on the mizzen, the coat on the mainsail is very badly secured, there are coats on the fore and mainmasts, probably to prevent their becoming covered all over with sticky china clay dust, but it was most unusual to coat masts in this way. On the other hand, in loading or discharging china clay it was the custom to cover up the lanyards and rigging with old bags up to about six or seven feet, as otherwise the clay would stick to the pine tar with which the natural fibre ropes were dressed as a preservative. This has not been done. Note that the planking up to a strake down below the clearly visible loadline has been sheathed over with an extra layer to lessen leaks and help to keep her together despite rotting frames – a sure sign of an old vessel. Yet the *Susan Vittery* lasted until 1953 when she was lost at sea, still working at least 30 years after this photograph was taken. (National Maritime Museum)

20 This photograph of the *Susan Vittery* at sea was taken many years after that in the last Plate. Notice how her squaresails have been changed from a single topsail stowed in the bunt (the centre of the yard) in the manner of the 1860s (or of H.M.S. *Victory*) with a standing topgallant above to double topsails on a much shortened topmast and without the topgallant. She had been given a big whaleback wheelhouse. Notice also the squaresail set flying under the foreyard, used when off the wind. (National Maritime Museum)

21 LEFT The *Two Sisters* of Bideford. The next three photographs show the schooner *Two Sisters*, registered as of the Port of Bideford at the time the photographs were taken. She was built at Bosham on Chichester Harbour in Sussex in 1882. Bosham is now a busy yachting centre. Then it was a creek village with coal cargoes coming and grain cargoes going out in schooners and ketches. The *Two Sisters* was built slowly and this first photograph shows her stern showing between the trees as she lies on the slip of the rural shipyard. (National Maritime Museum)

22 The *Two Sisters* was a narrow, shallow, vessel with a long main boom and big transom counter. This photograph shows her just arrived in Dover Harbour, her starboard anchor has been let go, the main topping lift has been set up, preparatory to lowering the mainsail, the boat has been put over the side to clear the hatchway for the crew to stow the foresail and a seaman is unhooking the burton. She has a new boom jib and a crew of five and is, of course, deep laden. This is another of Mr Amos' splendid photographs. (National Maritime Museum)

23 This photograph shows the shape of the *Two Sisters*' hull as she lies on the mud of a tidal harbour. She has either arrived on the last tide or is to sail on the next as the sail covers are off and the peak halyards hooked on to the gaffs. There is a spiritlessness about this scene – the main sheet is in a tangle at the boom end, the sails are carelessly furled and the yards braced anyhow. These were the hard times of the late '20s or early '30s and shortly after it was taken she was laid up at Par in Cornwall and eventually sold to become a houseboat. While she was laid up at Par I saw her and as a child first became conscious of the interest of these last wooden sailing ships, so perhaps she was the genesis of this book. (National Maritime Museum)

24 The *Mary Ann Mandal* was built at Ulverston, Cumbria, in 1868. She was lying almost becalmed early one morning in March 1918 off the coast near Littlehampton. Just as the eastern sky was brightening a submarine was seen to break water a few hundred yards away. She surfaced until her decks were fully exposed and then attacked the schooner with rifle fire from the conning tower. Under the scheme of 1917 for the general arming of merchant ships the *Mary Ann Mandal* was equipped with two three-pounder guns. Lying nearby her in the morning calm was another well-known schooner, the *Mary Sinclair* equipped with two 12-pounders. The two sailing vessels at once returned fire.

This seems to have surprised the submarine, which promptly submerged. Some little time later she surfaced again a considerable distance away and attacked the schooners with a four-inch gun. The battle began in earnest and lasted for more than an hour, the submarine firing over 60 shots. The *Mary Ann Mandal* received a direct hit which destroyed her maintopmast and damaged the lower mast. Close shots, splinters and shrapnel soon began to wreak havoc on the decks and rigging.

But the sailing vessels held their own and the submarine remained at a relatively safe distance. Eventually an armed trawler came steaming at full speed and the U-boat submerged and did not reappear.

To hold their own in such an unequal battle of course reflected enormous credit on the crews of the two schooners. (National Maritime Museum)

25 This photograph of the *Via* built at Brixham, Devon, in 1864 and employed at times in the Newfoundland trade, at first sight suggests a handsome vessel. In fact she is an old treadmill. The weight of her huge mainsail and boom and gaff requires three blocks on her main gaff, instead of the usual two; she has no flying jib and is being sailed with her standing and boom jibs almost aback. Her upper topsail is repaired with secondhand canvas, some of which has advertising lettering on it. The old vessel was lost off the Irish coast in the summer of 1931. (National Maritime Museum)

26 The sails of the *Pet*, built in Scotland in 1876, are also old and patched but well cut and set, though the gaff topsail with its tiny jackyard is too small to be of much use and has the look of having been made for another vessel. Notice that she is the first vessel so far illustrated to have four shrouds to her mainmast, necessary because she was a big-built heavy vessel and liable to be laboursome and hard on her gear in a big sea. She made many deep-water voyages, but was eventually wrecked near Wick in the winter of 1931. (National Maritime Museum)

27 This is a lovely photograph of a very handsome vessel. The *Hilda*, shown lying in the Bridgwater River, was built at Connah's Quay, Clwyd, in 1893 and with her big sheer, straight sloping stem and clean narrow bows, numerous flat floors, shallow draught and pointed stern with none of the weight of the vessel carried abaft the stern post, she was absolutely typical of many vessels built between the Dee and the Clyde. These were the most practical of all British sailing vessels for the home trade in tidal water, since with their flat floors and almost no drag – the keel was parallel with the waterline when the vessel was afloat and not a foot or two deeper at the stern than the bow as with the keels of many schooners – they could be laid on the ground in any suitable berth. They could sail without ballast, which gave them great economic advantage, since they did not have to load it and discharge it each time they sailed without a cargo, and because of their simple shape they tended to be long lived. These 'Barrow flats', as they were called in Appledore, were very practical and successful vessels. This photograph was taken by Mr W Sharman in Bridgwater about 1910. (National Maritime Museum)

28 By way of complete contrast, here is another flat-floored shallow-draught vessel but of a very different kind. In the nineteenth century a number of big sailing vessels were built on the lines of London River sailing barges with flat bottoms, hard chines, straight stems and leeboards, one on each beam, which served the same function on a huge scale as the centre plate of a racing dinghy. They were intended principally for the coal trade from the North East coast to the shallow south east coast ports and the small villages on Portsmouth and Chichester Harbours, but some of them went much further afield. This one, the *Friendship*, built at Sittingbourne in Kent in 1890, had a deadweight tonnage of about 400. She was rigged as a three-masted staysail schooner, an unusual rig in Britain though some vessels from Porthmadog were similarly rigged, and she is shown leaving Dover in tow – the tug is out of the picture – while sail is being set. She was lost in collision with a steamer in the Humber before the First World War. (National Maritime Museum)

29 The noble *Alert* was one of the finest of British schooners. Built at Runcorn in 1885 she was converted to be a twin-screw auxiliary motor yacht in 1938 but broken up during the Second World War. She sailed many times to Newfoundland, to Mexico and the Mediterranean. Here her upper topsail yard is lowered on to its lifts, as was the custom when a schooner was in port. She is light – she has no cargo – and her loadline is well out of the water. (National Maritime Museum)

30 The *Alert* like many schooners had a traditional figurehead, in this case white painted, female, with crossed hands pressed to her breasts. Note the chain of the bobstay running aft to the port hawse hole. This is loose while the vessel is in port. When sail is set it will be tightened up on the windlass. This will haul down the end of the bowsprit and tighten up the foremast stays and therefore the luffs of the standing jib, the boom jib and the flying jib, which are set from them. (National Maritime Museum)

Fowey Harbourmouth

Valentine's Series

31 This photograph has been included especially because it shows a rather unusual type of sail – the pair of triangular sails set above the topsail in place of a topgallant sail. Sails of this kind were probably used by only a few score vessels in the late nineteenth and early twentieth centuries. The vessel, shown sailing out of Fowey, is Cornish built, from the look of her, but her forestay comes down half way back to the pawl bit, the flying jib stay comes to the topmast just above the upper topsail yard instead of going right up under the truck; the main topping lift is down to the eyes of the rigging at the mainmast instead of up on the cap. The photograph is very old – there is almost no building on the headland above Polruan and by early in the present century all vessels were towed out of the harbour by a steam tug. (National Maritime Museum)

32 I was born and grew up on the Somerset coast of the Bristol Channel and one of the commonest sights of childhood was schooners or ketches sailing up and down on the tide. This photograph was taken from the path which runs along the low cliffs and shows a very typical sight, the *Dispatch*, built at Garmouth in 1888 and owned at the time the photograph was taken at Saul, Gloucestershire, romping along light with a flood tide and a strong breeze carrying her up towards Sharpness. (National Maritime Museum)

33 Many references have already been made in this book to the export of dried and salted cod fish, known as 'stockfish', in schooners from the Outports of Newfoundland and the creeks and cracks in the rocks of the Labrador to the Mediterranean and northern Europe.

This photograph shows Venison Tickle in Labrador with three local schooners and a three-master which, from the general look of her, might be Danish. She appears to be loaded and her foretopmast has been sent down with its yards, presumably in the course of repairs.

More salted cod is drying on the 'flakes', the wooden structures in the foreground, and yet more on the open beach, where three men are tending it – inspecting it for progress in drying and turning it over.

From little cracks in the rocks like this, thousands of tons of cod fish were exported to Europe in schooners between 1870 and the Second World War. (Public Archives of Newfoundland)

34 The dried and salted cod fish industry still continues on a reduced scale and fish are still exported from Canada and consumed in parts of North America. In some areas this poor man's staple food for 400 years is now a delicacy on sale in supermarkets. Salt fish can be bought at specialist delicatessens in England and is delicious if properly prepared – but this is a long job for the cook.

I took this photograph in the autumn of 1978. It shows cod drying in the sun and wind on flakes on the south shore of the Gaspé Peninsula in the Province of Quebec, Canada. Much salted cod nowadays is steam-dried and salted under controlled conditions in fish factories. A sight such as this is now becoming very rare. (Basil Greenhill)

35 There have also been a number of references in this book to the three-masted schooners built at Porthmadog between 1891 and 1913 which represented the finest development of schooner-rigged vessels in Britain. There were 32 of them and one barquentine, all closely similar in appearance, with very tall masts usually of the same height, like a Canadian tern schooner (see the next section of this book), but, unlike a Canadian tern schooner, with very square (long) yards on the foremast. They all had double topsails and a standing topgallant sail. As to the hulls, they had big shoulders, were high in the floors at the bow and stern and had long flat sections amidships which gave them cargo-carrying ability. They had a very marked sheer, particularly they rose steeply forward of the foremast which gave them a high bow for going over a sea.

This is the *Dorothy*, built at Porthmadog in 1891, one of the first of these vessels, shown towing up the floating harbour at Bristol with a P & A Campbell pleasure steamer in the background. (National Maritime Museum)

36 The hull form of one of the later Porthmadog schooners is shown very well in this photograph of the *David Morris*, built in 1897 and wrecked in November 1924. She is lying at low tide on a bank of the river Parret, the Bridgwater River, in Somerset. (National Maritime Museum)

37 Other than the later Porthmadog schooners the most famous later British vessels customarily employed in the Newfoundland stockfish trade were the smaller schooners belonging to John Stephens of Fowey and Par, in Cornwall, and his family.

This photograph shows the Stephens' schooner *Little Gem* lying in a Newfoundland harbour where she is loading saltfish at a long wooden finger wharf. Note the studding sail booms on her foreyard. These little schooners were the last British merchant sailing vessels regularly to carry studding sails on deep water, which they did until 1917. Studding sails were additional sails set on booms rigged out beyond the ends of the yards. They were carried by tea clippers and some other vessels in special trades in the earlier part of the nineteenth century and before. (National Maritime Museum)

38 This very handsome vessel is the *Sidney* built by R Cock & Sons at Appledore in 1897. She was employed in the Newfoundland trade, but this photograph was taken off Dover by Mr Amos probably in the 1920s from the dory he bought from a French Newfoundland Banks fishing schooner. (National Maritime Museum)

39 The last British schooner to sail in the Newfoundland stockfish trade was the *Lady St John's*, built at Kingsbridge in Devon in 1898, which between 1924 and 1926 made five easterly passages across the North Atlantic in an average of 29 days, including one from St Johns to Oporto of only 14 days. In 1928 her three eastward passages averaged 18½ days.

The *Lady St John's* was the last British merchant sailing vessel in a very hard sailing vessel trade which had continued uninterrupted for four and a half centuries. She made her last passage in 1930. This photograph shows her lying in St Johns in the 1920s with three members of her crew leaning on her rail. (Public Archives of Newfoundland)

40 This schooner is under construction at David Williams' yard at Rotten Tare, Porthmadog, and is very probably the Newfoundland and Labrador trader *M A James* of 1900. David Williams himself is second from the left with his yard gang lined up around him. The spikes sticking out of the sides of the vessel are the ends of the treenails, wooden pins which were used as fastenings to secure the planks to the frames in many schooners including this particular class of vessel built in this part of Wales in the early years of this century. They will be cut off when the planking is complete. I have a section of one of the *M A James'* planks in front of me as I write. The treenail holes are still there, as is a fragment of the yellow metal sheathing with which she was covered below the waterline to protect her from marine organisms which eat into wood. (Gwynedd County Archives)

41 Here David Williams is wearing a sun helmet. Part of the ceiling, the inner lining of planks, is being fitted, probably in the same vessel as in the last plate. At David Williams' yard the deck beams were not fitted until after the lower part of the ceiling. The more usual building practice was to complete the whole framework of the vessel including the deck beams and then to plank and finally to fit the ceiling. (Gwynedd County Archives)

42 The seams between the planks were caulked, that is plugged with oakum (natural fibre) rammed in with special irons driven with special caulking mallets and then sealed off on the outside with pitch, ideally to a depth of the breadth of the outside of the seam. Here three shipwrights, the brothers Goss of Calstock in Cornwall, are working at renewing the caulking of an old vessel. One holds an iron and a mallet, another has his mallet under his arm. The basket is full of oakum, teased out hemp fibres, which will have to be rolled into strands on the knees of the men before use. (National Maritime Museum)

43 A three-masted schooner needed about one hundred blocks in her rigging. Their manufacture was a special trade, virtually an industry on its own. There is still one working block shop left in the world, the Dauphinée blockshop at Lunenberg, Nova Scotia, established to serve the great fleet of fishing schooners which sailed from this historic Canadian port until the Second World War. This photograph was taken in Philip Green's blockshop at Appledore, North Devon, where the blocks for the *Annie Reece* (Plate 48) were made, in the early years of this century, and it shows recently manufactured three part, two part and single part blocks of different sizes. The deadeyes and bulleyes for the rigging were also made in this shop. (National Maritime Museum)

44 A great deal of special ironwork went into the construction of a schooner, the mast ironwork, the castings for the windlass and cargo winch, the ironwork for the pumps, the iron fastenings, if she was not fastened with yellow metal, or like the *M A James*, with treenails and yellow metal. The workshop shown here, John Beara's at Appledore, made much of this material, as well as stoves for vessels and houses but specialised in the manufacture of the complicated Williams' patent roller reefing gear with which a number of the British schooners and many ketches, pilot boats, and contemporary yachts and sailing boats were fitted. The photograph was posed to show different stages of the manufacture of this gear. (National Maritime Museum)

45 Here is the *M A James*, shown under construction in Plates 40 and 41, in her old age, her topmasts reduced and without her yards, but still a very handsome vessel, making a good deal of money for her last owners, the Slade family of Appledore. Smoke from the auxiliary diesel engine with which she was fitted when her rigging was reduced in 1930 can be seen around the foot of the mizzen mast. The *M A James* was the last of the late Porthmadog Newfoundland trade schooners to survive; she was broken up at Appledore after the Second World War. (W J Slade)

46 RIGHT, ABOVE I have included this photograph, despite its poor quality, because it is the only surviving visual indication of the accommodation in a British schooner built for the Newfoundland trade. It shows the day cabin shared by the master and mate of the *M A James*. Built into the stern of the vessel, it was triangular in shape with lockers built into the walls above a shelf which backed a bench around a triangular shaped table, the after part of which is visible in the photograph. Here, in the democratic society of a merchant schooner, all the crew including the master and mate, ate their meals in relays.

I took this photograph in 1946 when the *M A James* lay derelict at Appledore after having been neglected and ruined when on naval service in the Second World War. (Basil Greenhill)

47 RIGHT In the late nineteenth century and the early years of the present century, a number of steel schooners were built at different places in Britain and some in Ireland. Others were bought from abroad and they successfully competed in the home trade and on deep water with the traditional wooden schooners. The identity of the vessel in this photograph is not absolutely certain but she is very probably the *George B*

Balfour, built at Carrickfergus on Belfast Lough by Paul Rogers in the 1880s and owned by James Fisher & Sons of Barrow-in-Furness, who owned more schooners than any other owners in Britain. During the 70 odd years of its existence as a sailing-ship-owning concern the company managed a total of 132 vessels. (Basil Greenhill Collection)

48 The *Annie Reece* was built by R Cock & Sons of Appledore, North Devon, in 1909, one of a trio of steel schooners, the others were the *W.M.L.* and the *Lucy Johns.* Notice that she does not have the gaff jaws used on all wooden vessels so far illustrated but some sort of patent arrangement like those rigged on some gaff yachts. I do not know how long she kept this gear but it looks as if it might well jam. The photograph was taken by a member of the Cock family in 1909 while the new vessel was having her first coat of paint and her new sails were being bent. (National Maritime Museum)

49 A number of foreign-built schooners were bought by British owners and run in the British home trade and on deep water, usually successfully. This steel vessel was built at Hammelwarden, Germany, by Carl Lühring as the *Weser* and under the British flag was re-named *S F Pearce*. The photograph shows her at a late stage of setting sail – the flying jib is still being hauled up, the mizzen sheet has not been properly cleared, the fore lower topsail has not been properly sheeted home. The port anchor is just breaking water – she has evidently set sail from anchor – and, of course, the running bobstay has not yet been hauled tight on the windlass. (National Maritime Museum)

50 The *Ingrid* was built by a group of local farmers in Geta Parish in the Åland Islands in the Finnish Archipelago in the mouth of the Gulf of Bothnia in 1906/7 for employment in the timber trade to Western Europe. She was very successful, sailing as well to the White Sea, Montreal, the Gulf of Florida, and the West Indies. She was bought by British owners in 1919, the only Åland-built vessel ever to pass under British registration, renamed *Rigdin* and sailed to the West Indies and in the home trade, latterly rerigged as a barquentine. She was one of the last three square-rigged merchant sailing ships registered as of and sailing from a home port in the United Kingdom. She is shown in this photograph in Lorient during her maiden voyage. (Ålands Sjöfartsmuseum)

51 A number of Danish- and Swedish-built schooners were bought by British owners. This vessel is not actually a schooner but a ketch, a galeas (*galease* in Danish) as ketch-rigged vessels are known in this south part of the Baltic, built at Lysekil north of Göteborg in southern Sweden in 1921 as a demonstration vessel for the Scandia Engine Company and on the lines very popular with contemporary Danish builders. She was first named *Jules Claes* and renamed *Dido C* by her British owner, Stephen G B Chugg of Braunton, North Devon, who bought her in 1924 in Brussels. I took the photograph at Braunton in 1940. The cargo was being discharged into two-wheeled horse carts which each took a few basketfuls of the Forest of Dean coal she had brought down from Lydney in Gloucestershire. This kind of maritime rural scene was common until the Second World War anywhere around the coasts of Britain. All seagoing trade of this kind has been obliterated by the development of road transport. (Basil Greenhill)

52 Some big wooden three- and four-masted schooners were taken up by British owners in the late nineteenth and early twentieth centuries for employment in various deep water trades. Almost all of them were built in North America, a few steel schooners in Britain.

This photograph shows the *A B Sherman* built at Boston in 1883 as a three-master and employed by her American owners in the coal trade from Virginia to Baltimore and Philadelphia with occasional timber cargoes from Georgia to New England.

Shortly before the entry of the United States into the First World War, she was caught by a British naval patrol supplying fuel to a German submarine off the Scillies. After an exchange of gun fire she was brought into St Mary's by a British armed trawler, the *Nancy Lee*. She was towed to Plymouth where she was laid up until 1919 and then sold to owners in Fowey, Cornwall, by whom she was refitted and rerigged as a four-masted schooner.

She did not sail long for British owners. She was sold in 1923 to Italians after discharging a cargo of china clay at Leghorn. (National Maritime Museum)

53 One of the most famous of British schooners was the *Frau Minna Petersen*, later named *Jane Banks*, here shown, above, in her old age. Built at Porthmadog in 1878 by Simon Jones, she was a forerunner of the Porthmadog schooners of a generation later. She was first rigged as a staysail schooner and was named to please the German businessmen with whom her owners were working in the slate trade. She sailed as well to Smyrna, to the Danube, to the West Indies and frequently to the Mediterranean and Newfoundland. When owned by the Stephens family of Fowey she was one of the last two British schooners to make trans-Atlantic passages, to Bermuda and Jamaica in the 1920s. She was lost off the coast of Finland in 1944. The next six photographs were taken on board her at sea in the home trade, also in her old age, and they show details of the sails and rigging. With her pedigree, her world wandering and her long life, she might be taken as almost the archetypal British three-masted merchant schooner. (Graham Gullick)

54 On board the *Frau Minna Petersen*, later *Jane Banks*, at sea. The wind is fair but not dead astern so the foresail boom can be seen slacked off nothing like as far off as the other two, otherwise the sail would catch no wind at all. Notice the ratlines in the main rigging, which are of hemp line seized to the shrouds to enable the crew to go aloft. On the forerigging, however, serving the same purpose as the ratlines, can be seen wooden battens. They were used on the forerigging because in a vessel with squaresails on the foretopmast the crew were called upon to work aloft much more often on the foremast to loose or furl the sails, whereas the main and mizzen gaff topsails were sent up flying from the deck on a jackstay in the *Jane Banks* and there was no necessity to go aloft on these masts unless something went wrong, or for maintenance. (Captain J Raddings)

55 This photograph was probably taken at the same time as that in Plate 54. It shows the *Jane Banks* at sea in fine weather with very little wind. But although the sea is calm, blocks and tackles can be seen on the leeside of, and attached to, the ends of the fore and main booms, in opposition, as it were, to the fore and main sheets. These are preventer tackles (known to the crews of the west country schooners as 'kicking straps') to prevent the booms from swinging to and fro across the deck, a process which rolled what little wind there was out of the sails and caused expensive chafe and wear on the gear. The presence of these kicking straps indicates that when the photograph was taken there was a ground sea in which the vessel was rolling in the light breeze. The barrel of the dolly winch can be seen immediately forward of the stem of the white boat. Notice the washing drying in the lee main rigging.

Captain J Raddings, who took this series of photographs, noted 'my last trip (in the *Jane Banks*) from Par to London, Deptford Creek, we were 21 days, nearly drifted there, the freshest wind we had was in the Thames, when we beat up to Barking Reach, top end, where we had to go off the wind to clear a spreety barge, which should have given way. Couldn't get back on the wind, being flood tide, westerly wind, had to bring up just under Triplock Point, and tow up next tide.' (Captain J Raddings)

56 This photograph was probably taken from the end of the mizzen boom, Captain Raddings sitting there with his camera on the lee side of the sail.

Note the jaws of the main gaff, the spar to which the head of the mainsail is laced. Close to the jaws, on the under side of the gaff, can be seen a block carrying a single line, a white line leading down to the deck. This is the main gaff topsail sheet. The sheet leads to, and through, a sheave at the end of the gaff, at the peak, and this hauls out the clew of the topsail to the gaff end. By looking closely at the photograph you can see the tack of the main gaff topsail hauled down taut to about three feet below the gaff. It can be seen covering the gaff further up. The shadow of the lower part of this topsail shows on the mainsail.

Aloft and ahead of the other sails the square double topsails on the foremast are clearly visible, doing their work of pulling the vessel along. It was these sails that made the two- and three-masted British-style schooners among the most efficient small sailing vessels ever built for the work they did. On the port side can be seen the sheet attached to the clew of the lower topsail, and also the clew line of that sail, used to haul up the clew when the sail is taken in. (Captain J Raddings)

57 Once the squaresail was taken in it had to be made fast to the yard. This photograph, left, shows Captain Raddings who was a working member of the crew of the *Jane Banks*, on the lower topsail yard. He has just cast off the gasket, the rope with which the sail was secured to the yard when furled, and is shaking out the canvas on the sail in order that it should dry out while the vessel is lying at anchor in Fowey Harbour. He stands on a foot rope which has swayed out behind him as he leans over the yard. The foot rope is hidden by his legs, but one of the stirrups by which the foot rope is slung from the yard is clearly visible in the immediate foreground. Note the robust iron rod, the jackstay, to which the head of the lower topsail is secured.

The wire rope leading upward, attached to the chain at the yarn end, the yard arm, is the lift.

Captain Raddings wears no lifejacket and no safety harness. Such innovations would have been completely impractical. Mr Edmund Eglinton, who worked for years in these vessels in the 1920s, commented when he saw this photograph, 'Your readers should imagine what it would be like up there about 80 feet above the deck, with the ship plunging and cork-screwing below in wet and windy weather; everything slippery and jerking about, especially in the darkness of the night. To be cluttered up with a life jacket would be to invite destruction. An oilskin coat was also a hazard, it restricted agility and, should the wind get up inside by the updraft from a sail, one could be torn from the yard – or any other spar.' (Captain J Raddings)

58 This photograph, right, was taken from the bowsprit end, about 25 feet out from the stem of the *Jane Banks*, and in consequence she is foreshortened, but it does illustrate the heavy gear of the schooners. At the time Captain Raddings took this picture there were probably no more than four men on board, including the master. There may also have been a boy to do the chores of the cabin and galley, to trim and fuel the navigation lamps and also the cabin and fo'c'sle oil lamps.

Yet note the size of the chain to which the boom jib stay is attached and also the size of the chain necessary, with the clip hooks attached to the jib itself, to withstand the strain put upon it by that most important sail. The canvas of these sails was thick and heavy and when wet almost like board. Elbows, knees and boots were the best tools to tame it.

Notice the chimney of the galley (the cookhouse on deck) tilted outwards from the down draft of the sails. These funnels were always a problem. Every time the ship went about, the funnel had to be lifted off.

The white ropes in the foreground, one at each side of the picture, are wire stays running out to a spider band at the end of the bowsprit and the port one is rather slack because the vessel is on the starboard tack. The stirrup ropes attached to them are to support the bellies of the jibs when they are hauled down until someone can go out on the foot ropes of the bowsprit to furl them and make them fast. There is no safety net for the crew and nothing of the kind was ever carried in working schooners. (Captain J Raddings)

59 This photograph was taken from one of the yards on the starboard side. The wind is abeam, or nearly so, with a fresh breeze. Note the heavy towing hawser on the hatchway; it was probably a 10-inch rope and could have been a hundred fathoms long, very heavy work to pull in when the tug had cast off. Again the timber battens on the fore rigging can be seen clearly; they were safer and more kindly to bare feet than the ratlines shown on the main shrouds. The whale-backed house behind the man at the wheel, conspicuous in many photographs of British schooners in this book, usually had two compartments: one was the lavatory and the other a lamp and paint locker. (Captain J Raddings)

60 Three ketches being towed up the Bridgwater River in Somerset. To illustrate how much information can be gleaned from such an old photograph by a man who had depended on his work in such vessels for his living I quote the comments made by Mr Edmund Eglinton: 'This photograph was taken many years ago. One pointer to this is the fact that the topsails of all three vessels are tied up aloft and not set "flying" on jackstays from the deck. Another indication is that the booms of the mainsails have no patent reefing gear, the sails are loose-footed.

I feel that a tug master would have wanted a tow rope, a hawser [like that on the hatch of the *Jane Banks* in Plate 59], on the *Good Intent*, not the four inch warp that is leading from her starboard bow chock – even though there are two other warps leading to the other vessels and "stoppered" to each bow of the *Good Intent* – especially as two of the ships are fully loaded.

This set-up leads me to think the towing vessel may have been a friendly steam barge giving the three little ships a snatch in to their discharging berths, in other words they were inward bound.

Had the vessels been outward bound I should have thought the two astern of the *Good Intent* would have had all their sails set ready, as they would be the first to cast off their tow ropes.

If I am correct, then the sailor in the main rigging of the ship astern on the right hand side of the photograph, the *Marie Eugenie*, is tying up the topsail, not getting it ready to set. Probably the reason the *Good Intent* has not taken her topsail down is that it is set on the starboard side, not on the port side as are the other two. To take it down without fouling the peak halyards, it would be necessary to luff the vessel up, but the weather is obviously fine, so they may be waiting for a bend in the river bringing the vessel head to wind.

There may be only two men aboard the *Marie Eugenie* and as soon as the sailor in the rigging has finished with the topsail his very next job will be to slack away the anchor and lower it down to the hawse hole, it appears to be already off the rail. The other two vessels have their anchors hanging below the hawse pipes. There are five men and a boy aboard the *Good Intent*. Maybe the merchant and two hobblers [men employed to help moor the vessel when she reaches Bridgwater]. Their boat is probably under the vessel's stern.'
The *Good Intent* carried around her taffrail the text 'The Sea is His and He Made It'. She was built at Plymouth in 1790, and lasted into the 1920s. The *Marie Eugenie* was built at Regneville in France at an unknown date and owned in Bridgwater. (National Maritime Museum)

The North American Schooners

The schooner was really a North American creation. It was the settlers on the East coast who developed it into as efficient a way of rigging a small vessel as the technology of the period and their limited resources of capital, materials and manpower, allowed, and then they sailed it back to Britain and Europe.

Eighteenth-century schooners were probably never as handy as small brigs, but they cost probably less than half as much to rig initially and less than half as much to maintain and to man. This was a vital factor in a pioneer colonial community, some of whose members were still holding on to the edge of the wilderness by the tips of their fingers and toes. As technology improved and stronger, tighter-woven canvas became available to cut into flatter and more efficient sails, as ironwork and ropes improved, so the schooner became as efficient as the brig, and then more efficient because she could sail closer to the wind and she could come round more quickly when sailing on the wind.

So the schooner became the normal small merchant sailing vessel of the young United States and of British North America. Through purchase, which went on increasingly from the late eighteenth century, and through the ports which engaged in trades which employed small vessels sailing to North America, through the shipbuilding industry of Prince Edward Island, the schooner came back to Britain.

At the same time she grew in size, always pressing against the limits of what was technically possible. By the late eighteenth century three-masted schooners began to appear. Prince Edward Island produced its first three-master, the *Dispatch* in 1814 and by the 1830s they existed in some numbers. But it was after the awful upheaval of the War between the States that the schooner really began to develop in size in North America. After this conflict the United States, whose magnificent square-rigged ships had challenged British shipping supremacy in the 1850s, turned away from the sea. The Civil War had resulted in the destruction, sale or transfer to foreign flags, of nearly half the American deepwater merchant fleet. After the war the compound engine had been proved in British steamships and the international industrial situation showed that the future of shipping lay with steel and steam not with the wooden ships into which the great white pine stands of Maine had been so effectively converted. The high cost of steel precluded the building of a modern merchant fleet in America and American law effectively barred the building up of a fleet by purchase of foreign-built tonnage. At the same time the trans-Continental railroad was completed, the West was opened up and seemed to provide unlimited opportunities for capital and enterprise as did industrialisation and urban development in the east. People the world over have not taken to the sea in history if there are alternative occupations available on land offering equal or better opportunities. American enterprise turned inland and though for a short time big wooden square-rigged ships continued to be built in New England, particularly for the trade from the West coast to Europe, they were soon rendered obsolete by the development of British steel sailing ships and the triple-expansion engine for steamers in the mid-80s, which marked the real beginning of the end of the merchant-sailing ship.

There was little incentive anyway to build up a merchant fleet, since rapid industrialisation and phenomenal population growth absorbed most of America's tariff protected manufacturers, so there was relatively little export trade. Money and men turned to industry, railroads, real estate and to the West. There was only one trade which continued not merely to provide employment for a large number of vessels, but to grow. Under legislation dating back to the early years of the century, foreign flag vessels were not allowed to trade between American ports and neither were foreign-built vessels, even under the American flag. The coast trade consequently enjoyed a prolonged prosperity and for much of the nineteenth century and the first four decades of the twentieth, a greater tonnage of United States vessels was employed in coastwise than in foreign trades.

In the late nineteenth century the demand for coal for the new factories in New England, for the railroads and for domestic heating in the growing cities, and in due course for the production of domestic gas and electric power, all created a vast demand in New England which could only be satisfied from the mines of Pennsylvania and Virginia, mostly from West Virginia. The transport of coal gave rise to an enormous demand for shipping and it was in this trade that the schooner really came of age. The three-masters of the 1870s were quite unable to carry shipments of the size required, even though by European standards they were very big for the rig. The result was that four-masters began to be built in 1879, the first five-master was built nine years later, and twelve years after that, in 1900, the first six-master was launched. So the big schooner continued revolutionary development when all other forms of big merchant sailing ships were obsolete.

One of the big schooner's greatest advantages was, of course, that she was economical of manpower and there was the minimum of necessity to go aloft. At the same time, in 1879, as the four-master was introduced, came another very significant innovation, the introduction of the steam donkey engine in the *Charles A Briggs.* The steam donkey engine was used for hoisting sail and working the pumps and the anchors. It was the steam donkey engine which made possible the development of the five-master and the six-master. But the big schooner was probably at her best as a handy four-master of from 750 to 1,000 tons gross.

To understand the operation of these four-masters you must forget everything you have ever read of traditional sailing ship seamanship, the handling of the big square-rigged ships or the handling of the smaller British and European schooners. Her success depended on an approach to seafaring and ship management in many ways entirely different from anything that had ever gone before.

She needed only three or four skilled people and five or six ordinary seamen to handle her. A British schooner carrying an eighth as much cargo needed a crew half as big. A three-masted barque of the same cargo capacity needed two or three times the crew, a steamer even more men. And the crews of these other vessels had to be almost all skilled seamen, engineers or stokers. The essentials for the handling of the four-masted schooner were a first class master, a first class mate and a first class donkey-man. The Master navigated, watched the weather signs and took the decisions about the amount of sail carried, and he and the mate and perhaps one or two of the seamen did the jobs requiring special skills, like splicing ropes and repairing sails. The donkey-man nursed the steam winch which did all the hard work on board. He had to be a very skilled man since his winch in effect hoisted the sails and took them in, raised the anchor and worked the vessel in dock. Power always had to be available on call. As Captain Karl V Karlsson (Plate 98) who as a young man worked as a seaman in the four-master *Edward H Cole* on the American coast told us, 'The donkey man was an old Swede. He had steam on the donkey all the time. You rang a bell and the winch began to turn!' The steam-driven winch, as one authority has said, was the crew, the Master was the brain and the other men were the agents who cooked and cleaned and brought about the necessary connections between the steam winch and the ropes controlling the sails and performing the other functions on board.

In *The Illustrated American* of 1891 an article appeared which put the matter of the use of the donkey-engine very well:

> Coincident with the development of size and rig has been the introduction of still more remarkable changes in the equipment of schooners, 'big ships require big crews', might have been an axiom twenty years ago, but it is not now, at least it is not applicable to these big schooners. Ten or possibly twelve men is the biggest crew required by any of them. The work of double or treble that number of men is done by machinery. A schooner is badly equipped indeed, now, that does not carry an engine to weigh the anchor, hoist the sails, and trim the sheets. As a shipowner tersely expressed it, 'The engine does everything but reef the sails, that is what the men are carried for.'

Later, when reasonably reliable oil engines were developed early in the present century, they were substituted for steam donkeys, a further economy since they could be operated without the licensed engineer required for the steam-donkey engine.

The sail area of a four-masted schooner was not almost infinitely flexible like that of a British-style three-master with her square topsails and easily reefed small fore and aft sails, or that of a barque with a whole series of different combinations of sails, small and large, open to the Master. If the weather looked threatening, but uncertain, the Master of a British schooner could carry his sails, knowing that if it came on to blow, he could take in his squaresails, take in the gaff topsails and reef his fore and afters relatively quickly. The Master of a barque knew that he could relatively rapidly shorten down from his full 22, 23, or 24 sails and that at a pinch sail could be taken in in almost any normal weather conditions, should errors of judgement make it necessary for this to be done.

But the Master of a four-masted schooner was faced with an entirely different situation; he could take in his gaff topsails and some of his headsails, but after that the next stage was reefing or taking in his four huge gaff and boom sails. This was a big job, carried out largely mechanically with the donkey-engine, a process admitting of little flexibility. It could be done quickly but it could not be done in really bad conditions. If the sails were to be reefed the same process applied, because to handle such huge sails with a crew a large part of which was often relatively unskilled it was necessary to lower them altogether first and then bundle up the lower part of the sail in a reef while it was on deck and then reset the sail with the donkey engine. The whole process of taking in the huge gaff sails was made much easier by the presence of a series of 'lazy jacks', heavy lines stretching from the mast head to the boom, inside which the sail neatly fell (in theory and usually in good weather) when the gaff was lowered. Nevertheless, if the big fore and afters were not got in in time they never could be got in at all and the canvas could be damaged perhaps beyond repair, which was an extremely expensive matter. So the Master of a four-master had to be exceedingly weather-wise and had to look an even longer way ahead in making his decisions about what sail he should carry than most ship Masters.

The regular work aloft with the gaff topsails in these vessels for reasons which will be explained was exacting and difficult. In the four-masters the gaff topsails were jib-headed, the long luff held to the topmast with mast hoops. The lower part of the luff, where it stretched down below the mast cap was, however, not secured to a jackstay (as it was in the very much smaller British vessels when the topsail was stowed aloft and not set from the deck, as in the *Jane Banks*), and so, set on the lee side, it tended to blow away from the masthead, which considerably reduced its efficiency. In order to make it stand to its work the tack of the topsail had to be shifted to the weather side of the gaff between the peak halyards and the gaff itself. The shape and the setting of these sails can clearly be seen in several of the photographs in this section of the book.

The mastheads of these big schooners were joined together by the triatic or jump stay which was an essential part of the whole rigging system on the big schooners. The gaff swung below this stay; the luffs of the topsails were secured to the topmasts with hoops above it, so that the lower part of the sail had to be lifted over the stay, the sheet disconnected and reconnected, unshackled and shackled, each time the vessel went round through the wind with the topsails set. In effect, the topsail had to be clewed up and reset every time the ship went round. This meant that a hand aloft had to shift the heavy chain sheets, which (in the words of Captain Karlsson, who was speaking in English, and not in his native Swedish,) in the *Edward H Cole* were 'the same size as the anchor chain'. The seaman had to haul the tack over the triatic stay and toss the coil of the tack line down to deck with a cry of 'sheet home' each time she went round. This work aloft on the bare fore and aft rigged masts, with little hand hold, required considerable physical strength, confidence and dexterity. It was perhaps the most difficult of all regular work aloft in any big sailing ship, though the job of taking in the gaff topsail in a small British or Scandinavian ketch, jumping about in a seaway, was even worse.

The big schooners required special handling. With their huge flat-floored hulls and long straight sides they took some time to get under way, but, despite their weight, they stopped quickly when the wind was spilled from their sails. Because their simple and economical rigging did not present much windage they could, and frequently did, anchor, even on a lee shore to ride out bad weather. Because of the steam winch again, the anchors could be and were massive and with very heavy cables which made the technique relatively safe, particularly in the shallow waters of parts of the United States east coast. It is possible that the loss of the great steel seven-masted *Thomas W Lawson*, the largest merchant sailing vessel ever built, when her cables parted in a gale off the Scilly Isles was due partly to the fact that her Master was doing what he had done many times before in perfect safety on the New England coast, but that he had not allowed for the power of a full southwesterly gale in an exposed position on the east side of the North Atlantic.

Most of these big vessels were employed regularly in the coal trade, but taken as a whole they carried many other cargoes. Ice was carried from Maine to New York, Washington, Philadelphia and Baltimore, all of which ports provided return cargoes of coal to New England. They carried hard pine from Savannah, Georgia and from Jacksonville and Pensacola in Florida for building purposes in New England and for railway sleepers and for shipbuilding – coasting voyages which were in British terms as long in distance as a round voyage from Bristol to the Canary Isles. They carried coal and lumber to the West Indies and returned with sugar and molasses. They took coffee from Brazil to New England. There is a lovely description by Henry Hughes of Porthmadog in his autobiographical *Through Mighty Seas* of one of these coffee schooners:

Following in the *Cleopatra's* wake came an American coffee clipper, a 2,000 ton, four-masted fore and aft rigged sailing vessel, running between Rio and the northern states of America, carrying the world's most delicious coffee to the American people. They were lovely ships, and quite different from our idea of clippers – four tall masts, scraped and sun-bleached, looking much like ivory. On these were set but twelve sails made of perfect material known as American cotton canvas and sitting faultlessly. Their spars and sails were the envy of the world. Black hulls, white

deck fittings, and high bows gave them a business-like appearance; and they could sail.

He exaggerates as to size a little, but otherwise the description is excellent. The vessel is probably the *Doris* of Belfast, Maine.

Spruce lumber was sometimes shipped by schooner from Nova Scotia or New England as far as the River Plate and there was an enormous boom in this trade in 1889. Considerable numbers of schooners made trans-Atlantic voyages with lumber, oil in barrels or cases, tobacco or guano, returning with Welsh coal, or with salt for the New England fisheries or fruit for New York or Boston. In the year 1876 alone no fewer than 233 trans-Atlantic voyages were made by American three-masted schooners and there was scarcely a European port from the Baltic to the Mediter-ranean where they were not seen. These trans-Atlantic passages continued steadily through the generations until the last two were made by the four-masted *Helen Barnet Gring* and the five-masted *Edna Hoyt* just before the Second World War. A few East coast three- and four-masters made successful voyages to Australia and the Far East. One five-master from Maine rounded Cape Horn and she like many small and a few other large North American schooners was a centreboard vessel with a drop keel, like an enormous racing dinghy.

East coast-built schooners were bought by European owners, Danes, Åland Finns and Estonians, and some of these vessels were run with great success in the Baltic timber trade to Western Europe, a business for which they were highly suited. A few were bought by British owners for operation out of United Kingdom ports. As has already been said, of the latter some big three-masters built at New Bideford, Prince Edward Island, were operated by Welsh owners very successfully in trade round Cape Horn to the West coast of South America. Altogether between 1879 and 1921 besides over 1,500 three-masters about 446 four-masted schooners were built in the Eastern states, 45 five-masters and ten six-masters, and another 40 or so four-masters in eastern Canada. The great majority of the bigger vessels were built in the State of Maine.

The great East coast schooners were owned and managed in much the same way as the small British vessels. They were mostly run individually as single corporate enterprises, owned in 64ths with the shares spread perhaps between 40 people with a managing owner who was the inspiration of 'setting up a vessel', as the local saying had it. The shareholders were of two kinds, those actively involved in the shipping industry, brokers, shipbuilders, sailmakers, ship-chandlers, contractors, the vessel's Master, who profited from her operation in ways additional to the dividends or shares and the 'dry owners', who simply drew dividends. The latter could include business contacts as far away as the mid-West, New York businessmen, and people who summered in the beautiful Maine harbours where the vessels were built and sought sentimentally to identify with the neighbourhood by investing in vessel property.

Once settlement on a large scale began to develop on the West coast in the second half of the nineteenth century the Pacific coast lumber industry rapidly grew up in the States of Washington and Oregon and later in Canada and with it there developed an extensive shipbuilding industry. Once again in the 1870s and afterwards the schooner became the choice vessel in this area. According to figures published by Jim Gibbs in his book *West Coast Windjammers* derived from the researches of the late Dr John Lyman, some 138 four-masters, five five-masters and numerous three-masters were built between the 1880s and 1908. In the First World War boom 99 five-masters, 56 four-masters and three six-masters – as well as eight big three-masters – were launched on the West coast. This in total meant that more than twice as many five-masters were launched on the West coast of North America than on the east and the five-master might be considered to be a typical West coast vessel. But in fact of the 99 five-masters, most of them fitted with auxiliary engines of one kind or another, launched during the war boom no less than 45 were built for the French Government, together with nine of the four-masters. Four of the five masters and 19 of the four-masters were launched for Norwegian owners. The story of this great fleet of big schooners under European flags in the twentieth century has never been adequately told, but built mainly of Oregon pine, they were nearly all short-lived vessels, in some cases lasting only a few years. Nevertheless some of them, like the *Valborg*, the *Odine* and the *Gunn*, worked successfully for years in the Baltic timber trade to western Europe for Åland Island and Estonian owners.

The French vessels were ordered as a result of a mission to the United States by André Tardieu, a prominent politician of the era, who was sent to the United States in 1917 in the role of 'High Commissioner for War'. He asked for authority to negotiate 200 wooden transport schooners of about 3,000 tons with auxiliary motors. In fact many of the great fleet soon after the end of the war were up on the beach at Portstren, beyond the commercial port to the east of Brest, and there they stayed while the local children played around them (and dubbed them 'Tardieu's Fleet') until they were broken up for firewood, some as late as the Second World War. A few were sold to American owners and one lasted, laid up in Brooklyn, until at least 1938. One or two were sold to British owners. The *Astri I.*, built at Astoria, Oregon, in 1917 for Norwegian owners, already by 1921 was a fishmeal plant hulk off Brightlingsea on the Colne under the name of *Gloria*. Another, or perhaps she was the *Gloria*, still lay moored in the Thames as a great blackened hulk in 1946. A few years later she was abandoned in a Kentish creek.

West coast-built schooners were mainly employed in the lumber trade down the coast to California, across the Pacific with lumber to Australia and back with coal or with copper or phosphate from the Pacific Islands to the West coast or Hawaii. Quite rapidly the schooners built on the West coast began to develop away from the fashion of the East. They were built with full poops and raised topgallant forecastles like British square-rigged ships, although their crews were accommodated in deckhouse forecastles like those of the East coast vessels. Many of these West coast schooners were built without separate topmasts, so that each mast was one tall single pole, and many of them had a triangular sail on their aftermost mast instead of a gaffsail.

Just as in Prince Edward Island, Canada, schooners and barquentines were built entirely of spruce and successfully employed on prolonged service in world trade, although spruce was not a favoured material for shipbuilding, so these West coast vessels were built sometimes almost entirely of Douglas Fir, sometimes called Oregon Pine, a timber not regarded as ideal for shipbuilding purposes in Britain and on the East coast of North America. Yet they gave many years of profitable service in the trans-Pacific trade.

Captain Fred Klebingat, a historian of these West coast schooners, has drawn an interesting parallel between the operation of one of the big five-masted schooners built on the West coast and the operation of contemporary square-rigged ships. The five-masted schooner, the *Crescent*, could carry 1,659,000 board feet of lumber with a total crew of ten, while a German four-masted steel barque with a total crew of thirty-three could carry only 2,250,000 board feet. A wooden square-rigged ship carrying the same amount of lumber as the *Crescent* had a crew just twice as large.

One other type of schooner developed in North America into a class of its own. This was the Canadian 'tern' schooner, the three-master with her masts all the same height and the topmasts, fore and main gaffs and booms, and much of the rigging often interchangeable between the masts. The name 'tern' was taken from a poker term meaning 'three of a kind'. These vessels were built in Prince Edward Island, New Brunswick, and Newfoundland, but especially in Nova Scotia where the great majority of them were launched. They were employed in international trade to and from the United States and the West Indies and many of them in the stockfish trade from the Atlantic provinces, the Gulf of St Lawrence, and especially from Newfoundland and Labrador, to European ports. Altogether over 800 of these vessels were built. Some of the later ones, like the *Nellie T Walters* built at Shelburne, Nova Scotia, in 1920, were among the finest and most efficient sailing ships of their size ever built. Over the years 1922–27, taking passages both ways and including a 31-day passage in 1926, the *Nellie T Walters*' average trans-Atlantic passage was 22 days, and one of her runs was from Marystown, Newfoundland, to Oporto in only 14 days.

Here is a description of one of these Nova Scotian three-masted schooners written by the British maritime historian, Sir Alan Moore:

> A few days later we left Gibraltar in the afternoon and when clear of the harbour took a monitor in tow. While we were so doing one of the most beautiful vessels I have ever seen sailed into the Bay, rounded-to in her own length almost, and began to shorten sail. She was a Nova Scotiaman, the three-masted fore and aft schooner *Frances Louise*. She had a low, graceful hull painted black, a yacht-like counter, and a rounded cut-away stem. Her masts raked slightly and the mizen-mast was the tallest. Her spanker or mizen was really her mainsail, in that it was the largest of the three. All three sails and the fore staysail were laced to booms.
>
> Her bowsprit was horizontal, and she set a single jib. All her canvas was beautifully cut. She seemed the last word in sail and contrasted strongly with the Spanish brig which we saw a few minutes later.

The *Frances Louise*'s bowsprit was, in fact, steeved and what the author meant by a single jib is not clear, but all the essentials are here. The *Frances Louise* was built at Lunenberg, Nova Scotia, in 1917 and she and her sisters with the rounded stem and cut-away forefoot represented the last distinctive individual type of merchant sailing ship ever to be developed. They were products of the twentieth century and before it was a generation old they were obsolete.

61 Though the schooner developed in North America until the second largest wooden merchant sailing vessel ever built was rigged as a six-masted schooner, small schooners, some of them very like the first little two-masters continued to be used in North American waters as long as sailing vessels were used at all. In the Outports of Newfoundland in the present century they still used the two-masted schooner rig on little vessels which elsewhere in the world would have been rigged as smacks, and even open boats were rigged as schooners in the eighteenth-century style. This photograph taken at Eastern Tickle, Fogo, Newfoundland, shows several of these little vessels of varying sizes. (Public Archives of Newfoundland)

62 At the time the photograph was taken this vessel was owned in France and named *Madeleine Charles*. Her origins are not known, but she was certainly built down-east, that is somewhere between Connecticut, USA and Prince Edward Island, Canada, since her whole appearance, the shape of her hull, her simple two-masted rig without a foretopmast, the raking heart-shaped transom counter, are absolutely typical of the small schooners of this part of North America in the later nineteenth century. (The late H Oliver Hill)

63 A later small Canadian built schooner, the *Snow Maiden*, lying in Saint John, New Brunswick. She was built at Digby, Nova Scotia, in 1902 and rebuilt in 1923 in the same place. She was 70 feet long – rather smaller than the British-built ketch *Progress* illustrated in Plate 17 and of very similar general shape to the *Madeleine Charles* in Plate 62. Notice the iron steering wheel, typical of these small Canadian and American sailing vessels. She was owned on Grand Manan and spent her life in trade about the Bay of Fundy and adjacent waters. (W J Lewis Parker)

64 The 'pinky' with the bulwarks at her pointed stern cocked up into a cover for her rudder head which also served as a seat of ease and a boom crotch, her very simple two-masted rig with only one headsail, a very long main boom and a little pole from which no sail was ever set as a token main topmast, was one of the earlier forms of American schooner. She developed in the late eighteenth or early nineteenth centuries from types in use in colonial times and persisted as a merchant vessel in local trade and as a fishing vessel in New England and Canadian waters into the present century. Today pinkies are being built again as yachts. This one is the *Maine*, built at Essex, Massachusetts in 1845, a perfect example of a pinkie, photographed at anchor off Belfast, Maine. She was broken up at Jonesport, Maine, in 1924. (Peabody Museum of Salem)

65 The shipbuilding industry of Prince Edward Island, Canada, was unique in North America in that among the numerous kinds of vessels launched, mostly for export, from big square-rigged ships to small schooners for Newfoundland, there were many built in the generally preferred style of contemporary British schooners, destined for sale on the British tonnage market.

But these vessels nevertheless had marked characteristics of their own, broad, heavy, transom counters and full quarters, flaring bows and raking stems combined with rather shallow draught, all of which can be seen in this photograph of one of them, the *Topaz*, built at Charlottetown in 1860 by Robert Longworth, photographed lying at low water in the Bridgwater River in Somerset, England, and broken up in 1928.

She was first rigged with a single square topsail and a standing topgallant, but the latter had been discarded by the time this photograph was taken. In its place is a three-cornered sail in one piece (as opposed to the two three-cornered topgallant sails shown in Plate 31) from yard arm to yard arm. The halyard goes up through a traveller landed on the eyes of the topmast rigging, as was usual with a topgallant yard in a schooner. The traveller went up with the cringle of the rope of the sail thereby holding the cringle, the head of the sail, close to the mast. When it was not set this triangular sail could be stowed separately, as shown in the photograph, or stowed in with the topsail as convenient. (National Maritime Museum)

66 Small North American schooners were not always two-masted. Among very small three-masters was the *Souvenir*, a miniature in hull form of the big tern schooners of the early twentieth century and with an open rail in place of bulwarks, like some of the big United States four and five-masters. She was built at Meteghan River. Nova Scotia, in 1903 as a two-master and lengthened and re-rigged as a three-master some time after she was built. She was then 61 feet long – smaller than most British ketches. Shown in her old age, she is reported to have been a lovely vessel to handle. Notice the small dory used as a ship's boat. (Nova Scotia Museum)

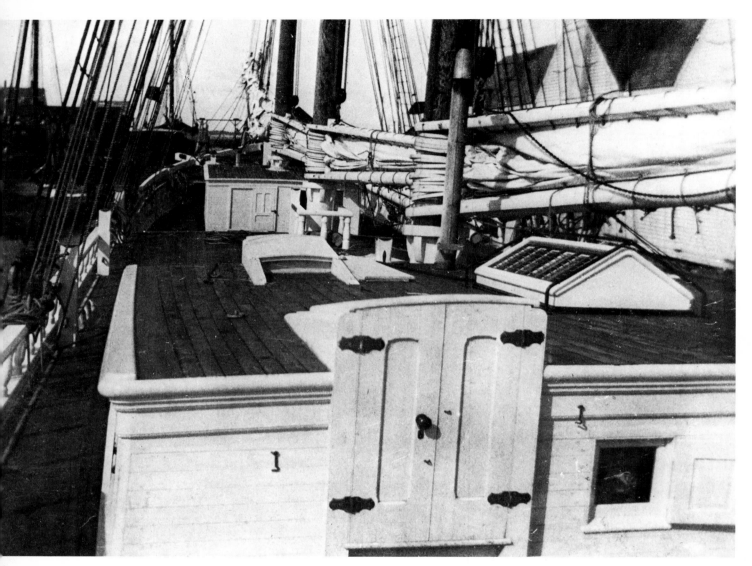

67 This a deck view in port of the three-master *Lavinia M Snow*, built at Rockland, Maine, in 1893. With her big deckhouse aft, like that of a Scandinavian barque, her deckhouse fo'c'sle, her rail and her 354 tons gross she is quite unlike the British three-masters illustrated in the last section of this book in size and general arrangements. (W J Lewis Parker)

68 Small schooners loading at one of the old wooden finger wharves, now all dismantled, at St John's, Newfoundland. They are taking a mixed cargo in drums, barrels, sacks, boxes and bales for the Outports, many of which were not accessible by road until recent years. Many have been abandoned as settlements, but some are still entirely dependent on sea transport – but now no longer by schooner. (National Film Board of Canada)

69 The *Margaret Thomas*, (see Plate 2) shown sailing on the port tack in a strong breeze, is a fine example of a big Maine-built four-master of the last period of building these vessels (apart from the boom of the First World War). She was built at Thomaston, Maine, in 1904. Notice the white-painted open rail used in many of these big schooners in place of the solid bulwarks usual in most types of sailing vessel. (National Maritime Museum)

70 This is one of the great photographs of a merchant sailing ship. It was taken by Fred Kitto of Fowey, England, and it shows the five-master *Rebecca Palmer*, built at Rockland, Maine, by Cobb, Butler & Co in 1901, 2556 tons gross, 260·4 feet long. She was the first five-master to cross the Atlantic, to Fowey in Cornwall where she loaded a cargo of china clay for New York City which she took back across the Atlantic in 32 days – a good passage for any sailing vessel. Palmer fleet records published by the historian of the big United States East coast schooners, Captain W J Lewis Parker USCG, show that the *Rebecca Palmer* paid out $126,784 in dividends to her shareholders in the first eight years of her life, which included this trans-Atlantic passage. (National Maritime Museum)

71 One of the most handsome of the bigger schooners was the *Cora F Cressy*, built by Percy & Small at Bath, Maine in 1902. She was of 2,499 tons gross and 273 feet long – the size of a contemporary steel four-masted barque like the famous *L'Avenir* which used to bring wheat cargoes from Australia to England in the 'grain race' before the Second World War. She could carry about 4,000 tons of coal from Virginia to Massachusetts and is supposed to have completed seven passages between these States inside 48 days. She had particularly high flaring bows which are still apparent in the vessel today (Plate 112) as she lies as a hulk at Bremen, Maine. (National Maritime Museum)

72 This is the mighty *Wyoming*, launched at the Percy & Small Yard at Bath, Maine (the site of which is now part of the Bath Marine Museum) in 1909 and the last six-master to be built. She was the second largest wooden merchant sailing ship ever launched, measuring 329·5 feet long, 50·1 feet in the beam with the depth of her hold of 30·4 feet. The photograph shows this huge vessel leaving the Kennebec River light, that is without cargo, on her maiden voyage. Sail is being set and the steam donkey engine is being used to set the sixth gaff sail, sometimes referred to as the driver. The *Wyoming* went missing at sea in 1921. (Bath Marine Museum)

73 This most interesting photograph shows a splendid contrast. The liner is the French *Normandie*; the four-masted schooner is the *Annie C Ross* built at Bath, Maine, in 1917 and later to become the last American four-masted schooner afloat. (National Maritime Museum)

74 The very comfortable living conditions for the Master and the mate of a big New England schooner. The vessel is the five-masted *Washington B Thomas* and the photograph was taken in her cabin shortly after her launch. Note the steam central heating unit in the middle of the floor, the phonograph, the high deck head and the pilasters on the panelled walls. The master, Captain William J Lermond, and his wife are seated facing the camera. The young man is their son. The vessel was tragically lost 53 days after launching when bound from Newport News with her first cargo of coal. Mrs Lermond lost her life in the wreck. (W J Lewis Parker)

75 This photograph, taken on board one of the last four-masters at sea, the *Helen Barnet Gring* launched at Camden, Maine in 1919, was made by Francis Bowker who was a member of her crew. He shows the long open main deck with the open rail in place of the bulwarks customary in other types of sailing vessel.

Notice that she has rigging screws in place of deadeyes and lanyards. Many of the later American, Scandinavian and Finnish schooners were fitted in this way, but very few British wooden vessels – in fact I know of only one, the ketch *Shamrock*, now preserved by the National Trust and the National Maritime Museum at Cotehele Quay in Cornwall. On the other hand, most later British vessels were fitted with roller reefing on the big fore and aft sails, a very labour-saving device which was never taken up by either Scandinavians or Americans. (F E Bowker)

76 A crew member on the cross-trees of one of the masts of the *Helen Barnet Gring*. This photograph shows the great size of all the fittings and of the wooden masts themselves. It was here that the difficult work of furling the huge gaff topsails had to be performed. Considering the difficulty of obtaining skilled hands to work these vessels in later years, and the relatively high degree of readiness to accept innovation shown by their enterprising owners, it is surprising some method of setting topsails from the deck without the necessity for work aloft at sea was not adopted (F E Bowker)

77 This superb photograph by Garret I Johnston of Long Branch, New Jersey, was taken in Perth Amboy and shows seamen at work bending a jib on the hanks on board the *Helen Barnet Gring.* It also shows the great size of the spars and fittings of a four-master.

The *Helen Barnet Gring* was lost off Cuba in 1940. Several models have been made of her. One is in the Maritime Museum at Göteborg in Sweden, another in the Mariner's Museum at Newport News in Virginia, and the third, one of the finest ever made of a big New England schooner, is on display in Gallery 14 of the National Maritime Museum at Greenwich, London. It was constructed in the Museum's Conservation Workshops from detailed information provided by Francis Bowker. (Garrett I Johnston)

78 The four-masted schooner *Joseph B Thomas* was built at Thomaston, Maine, in 1900 and in the early years of this century she took a cargo of boards across the Atlantic to Bristol in England. This photograph shows her towing down the Bristol Avon outward bound after discharging her cargo. It is a splendid deck view, conveying an excellent impression of simplicity of the rigging and fittings of one of these big East coast schooners. Her houses are half sunk into the deck, her low rail is open and her long open deck uncluttered with gear. Notice the rigging screws in place of dead eyes and lanyards and the enormous masts. The *Joseph B Thomas'* commander on this voyage was Captain Lermond, later to take charge of the *Washington B Thomas*, and who has been seen in Plate 74. (National Maritime Museum)

79 The five-masted schooner *Inca*, deep laden, is beating out of Puget Sound, State of Washington, towards the open sea. The wind and sea are both rising and her topsails have just been taken in. They are not properly stowed and are being allowed to blow about in a manner which can do them no good. It is possible that this is because her small crew have been employed in reefing the lower sails. Note the shoulder-of-mutton spanker, the poop from side to side of the vessel like that of a square-rigged ship, and the deck house forecastle merging into a full forecastle, also from side to side of the vessel, all of which distinguish the *Inca*, which was built at Port Blakeley, Washington, in 1896, from an East coast schooner. She was abandoned in the South Pacific in 1920 and subsequently towed to Sydney, Australia, and hulked. (Robert Weinstein)

80 The four-masted schooner *Fearless*, also photographed beating out of Puget Sound to sea, with a full deck load of lumber and fore, main, and mizzen gaffsails set with 'lumber reefs' to raise the booms clear of the deck load. The *Fearless* was built at Hoquiam in 1900 and, like the *Helen Barnet Gring*, was wrecked off Cuba, in her case in 1927. The photograph was taken in about 1912 (Robert Weinstein)

81 What a big deck cargo looked like on board a West coast four-master at sea. This photograph was taken on board the *Admiral*, built at North Bend in 1899 and wrecked on the notorious Colombia River bar in 1912. She is bound south to San Pedro from Bellingham, Washington, deep laden with Oregon pine (sometimes known as Douglas fir). The photograph was taken about 1905. (Robert Weinstein)

82 One of the 56 four-masted schooners built on the West coast during and immediately after the First World War boom for United States, Canadian, Norwegian and French interests was the *Gunn*, built at Victoria, British Columbia, in 1919 and shown discharging lumber in London, England. She was built for Norwegian owners, then owned in the Åland Islands of Finland and then sold to Estonian owners. For many years she operated successfully in the Baltic timber trade from the Gulf of Bothnia to Western Europe. (National Maritime Museum)

83 The *Lieutenant Granier* was one of the 45 five-masted schooners built on the West coast of North America during and just after the First World War for the French Government. She was launched by the Foundation Company of Portland, Oregon, in 1918, almost 260 feet long and equipped with twin triple expansion steam engines of 68 nominal horse power built by J W Sullivan of New York, with the furnaces and boilers exhausting through twin funnels, one on each side of the jigger mast. She was broken up in Scotland in 1924. (National Maritime Museum)

84 The five-masted *Jenny R Dubois* towers above the houses and sheds at Mystic, Connecticut, where she is about to be launched into a river only just free of ice. She was built on the upsurge of an industrial boom which followed the Spanish-American war of 1898. The consequent prosperity for shipbuilding and shipping lasted until 1904 and led, with other factors, to a great revival in the construction of big schooners to carry coal from Virginia to Boston. For some years it looked as if the great days of sail had returned in the eastern United States, but in 1908 there was a disastrous depression and this, together with the successful employment of steamers in the coal trade in the same year marked the end of the large-scale construction of big schooners in the United States, apart from the war boom which began nine years later. (Mystic Seaport)

85 The big down-east schooners were sometimes loaded in strange berths. This is the four-master *Charles A Dean* of Boston loading plaster at a wharf at Walton on the Minas Basin, Nova Scotia. Twice a day as the tide went out and left the Minas Basin almost dry the *Charles A Dean* grounded on the hard red mud, so that her keel, some of her frames amidships, and the wharf, took the huge weight of the big vessel and her cargo when she was loaded. This photograph shows well the powerful hull form of one of the big schooners. (W J Lewis Parker)

86 Four two-masters, two three-masters and three four-masters, lying in Bangor, Maine. The four-masters are the *Wesley M Oler*, the *Jennie S Butler* and the *King Phillip*. The photograph was taken before 1898, when the latter was lost in a gale. (W J Lewis Parker)

87 The Canadian tern schooner *Empress*, built at Montague, Prince Edward Island, by George Whiteman in 1901 and sold to owners in Barbados in 1913. This photograph was taken in Montague where she was lying in the summer of 1902. She was employed principally in the West Indies trade. The vessel under construction in the background is the *Janie F*, a two-masted schooner which lasted until the 1930s, and the little schooner being built in the foreground is the *Martha B*, only 37 feet long, built and owned by Felix Peters of Montague Bridge and employed in the local trade around the Island and the adjacent mainland. She was broken up in 1940. (Provincial Archives of Prince Edward Island)

88 The tern schooner *Edith M Green* was launched in 1917 from the yard of B N Melanson of Gilbert's Cove, Nova Scotia, watched by an excited crowd, most of whom seem to have arrived in T Model Fords. She was sold to French owners and renamed *Suzaky*. Notice the lads in the cross-trees of the foremast. (Nova Scotia Museum)

89 The *Nellie T Walters* was a fine example of the last type of merchant sailing vessel ever to be developed, the Nova Scotian round-stemmed tern schooner. Fast, handy and handsome she herself was a highly successful vessel in the salt fish trade across the Atlantic to Europe. Built at Shelburne in 1920 with Captain T Walters as master and a shareholder and named for a member of his family, when she was first sailed she amazed the local people by her handiness and speed. After many crossings of the North Atlantic she was lost on a passage with coal from Sydney, Nova Scotia, to Trinity, Newfoundland in 1939. This photograph shows her on the slipway before she was rigged. The round stem and generally yacht-like hull can be seen clearly. (Nova Scotia Museum)

90 Another type of Canadian three-master altogether. She is an unknown three-masted Great Lakes schooner, an example of a specialised vessel which played a very important part in the development of industry and settlement in Canada and some of the northern states of the United States. She has a straight stem and many details in her rigging which were peculiar to these vessels. She is shown being towed into Toronto by the tug *J D Schofield*. Toronto port regulations required vessels to be towed whether the wind was favourable or not. (Nova Scotia Museum)

The Life Story of a Schooner–

the *Bertha L Downs* later *Atlas*

The later big American schooners were constructed under conditions very different from those in the rural shipyards and shipbuilding places of western England and Wales in which the great majority of British schooners were born. The British vessels were built as vessels had been built before the Industrial Revolution. In most cases the men worked with their own tools right through the building of the ship and there was no power equipment in the yard. Everything was done by hand. They laid the keel and framed and planked up. Often they did the inside joinery, stepped the masts and helped with the rigging. They were employed by the yard and took their orders from the yard management, or they were employed for the building of the one vessel by the entrepreneur who organised and financed her construction at a shipbuilding place. By way of contrast many of the big American schooners were products of quite a different approach to shipbuilding; they were children of nineteenth-century industrial methods and were the only big wooden merchant sailing ships ever built in relatively highly-capitalised and well-mechanised big yards.

The New England Company yard at Bath near the mouth of the Kennebec River in Maine, where the *Bertha L Downs* was built had extensive machinery driven in the contemporary style by shafting and belting and several electric motors totalling some 140 horse power. Other big yards at Bath had covered saw mills with both circular and jib saws and powered planers. There were separate treenail-making shops with power driven treenail lathes which could turn out the 20,000 treenails required for a big schooner quite quickly. There were large blacksmith shops capable, with the use of some power drills, of handling the 300 or 400 tons of iron and steel which went into the building of a big schooner. It was used for bolts, nails, chain plates, mast ironwork and the massive steel reinforcing straps which, let into the frame faces before planking, strengthened the long narrow hull against the huge stresses set up in it, not only when sailing but when simply lying afloat laden with cargo. These straps were often nearly an inch thick and four inches wide and several thousand holes had to be drilled in them.

There were separate oakum shops in some yards which were the headquarters of the caulkers. A big four-master had about six miles of seaming to be caulked, and on a basis of four threads to each seam, each thread divided into loops, about 48 miles of oakum had to be spun and driven, work for 12 to 15 men working a six day week for approximately three months.

To build these big schooners timber was needed in prodigious quantities. The big five-masters, for instance, had keelsons 7 feet high and 8 feet wide at the base, made up of 14 × 14 inch baulks of hard pine. The lower masts were 120 feet long and over 2 feet 6 inches in diameter at the step. The topmasts were the size of the mainmast of a small British or Danish ketch. Most of the early big schooners had built-up masts made from many pieces of timber and bolted together, or bound with iron bands, but by the time the *Bertha L Downs* was built in 1908 the single stick Oregon pine masts came on flat railway cars right across the continent from the West Coast and were delivered by a branch line along the street right to the yard door.

The rest of the lumber came from all over the eastern states. Hackmatack was cut up in Aroostook County of Maine and sent down by rail to the shipyards. Timber contractors were supplied with moulds by the yard and these moulds were taken in schooners down to the southern states where individual frames were roughed out from the newly felled timber where it lay in the woods of derelict plantations in Virginia and eastern Delaware. Hard pine came down east from Georgia and South Carolina in schooners.

Most of the labour answered to contractors, not to the yard management. The contractors used the yard facilities but built up, paid and controlled their own labour gangs and they themselves were not employees of the yard. The greater part of the labour force of the yard therefore did not regard itself as attached to the yard with local loyalties, as in the small British yards, but as skilled craftsmen who might work anywhere where work was offering. This contracting system applied to the caulkers, the blacksmiths, the riggers, the painters and the men who, with schooner-building on the scale on which it was conducted in Maine at times in the late nineteenth and in the early years of this century, were able to make a good living simply out of finishing the bevelling of the frames, dubbing them with adzes.

The four-masted schooner *Bertha L Downs* was built by these methods at Bath in 1908 by Edward W Hyde at the old New England Company yard. She was a very handsome vessel, 175 feet long and 716 tons gross. She was registered first at Newhaven, Connecticut, as owned by the Benedict Manson Marine Company and sailed principally in the lumber and coal trades from the southern ports to New England. In 1916, fairly early in the First World War boom, she was sold with other vessels of the Benedict Manson Marine Co. This

was at a time when the managers knew they would get a very good price for the vessel, though a little later, as events developed, they would have done even better.

The *Bertha L Downs* was purchased by her first Master, Captain Bob Wells, in the guise of the 'Bertha L Downs Shipping Corporation' of New York, and in turn sold at the height of the First World War shipping boom in December 1917 to Rederei A/S Trans of Copenhagen.

This company renamed her the *Atlas* and employed her after the Armistice of 1918 in the timber trade from the eastern Baltic to west European ports until 1923 when she was sold to Arthur Ekbom of Mariehamn in the Åland Islands of the Finnish Archipelago, and again a few years later to Arthur Andersson of Mariehamn, both of whom employed her in the same trade. In 1931, when 23 years old and still in excellent condition, she was sold to Captain K Jurnas of Parnu in Estonia and became a unit in the remarkable Estonian fleet of big wooden multi-masted schooners employed in the Baltic timber trade to western Europe until the late 1930s.

The *Atlas* persisted in this work until the Soviet invasion of the Baltic states. She was taken over by the Russians and is said to have been sunk near Riga in 1942. She was raised by the Germans in the following year and, as with many Baltic States' vessels, her subsequent history is difficult to trace. She was renamed *Prindsesse Alice*, which would suggest Danish ownership, but no official record of this has been found in Denmark. She ended up in Kiel where she was broken up at the age of 40 in the summer of 1948 – one of the longest-lived, if not the longest-lived as a working vessel, of all the big North American schooners.

Captain Karl V Karlsson of Vårdö in the Åland Islands was her Master in her years under the ownership of Arthur Andersson. He told me in 1977 that she was extraordinarily well-built, the finest wooden ship he had ever sailed in or seen, and he had spent the greater part of his seafaring life in such vessels. Her planking was all pitch pine and no length in it was less than forty feet. Her ceiling was of 14 inch square pitch pine and the keelson built up of 24 inch square Oregon pine baulks, bolted right through to the keel and built up six feet high. Her pinrails and deck fittings were all twice as big as in Baltic or West coast of North America-built vessels and all her gear was correspondingly massive. She was a far finer vessel than other American schooners in which Captain Karlsson had sailed for some years on the East coast of North

America. She had central heating aft and a galley three times as big as was usual, with a fresh water pump and 20 tons of fresh water carried in the tanks. Many vessels carried only 1 ton. She was fitted out aft with oak and birch panelling; her spanker boom was 57 feet long and she was very handy under sail especially when loaded. When in ballast it was difficult to get her to come round when sailing on the wind but when loaded he could get her round in nine minutes from start to finish. In the Baltic trade she carried a crew of 11 including a Russian engineer who was a wizard with the 18 h.p. one-cylinder utility American Buffalo winch engine, 'a real son of a bitch', as Captain Karlsson put it, used as the old steam donkey engines had been, for hoisting the anchors and the gaff sails and for working the cargo.

91 This photograph illustrates the construction of the big schooners. It shows the building, not of the *Bertha L Downs*, but of the *Rachel W Stevens*, another four-master, built in the same yard as the *Downs* ten years earlier and 20 feet longer, but of similar construction and also owned in Connecticut. Note the massive size of the frames and the huge keelson built up of eight baulks of pine scarfed together. (W J Lewis Parker)

92 The *Bertha L Downs*, completed and ready for launching into the Kennebec from the old New England Company yard at Bath, Maine, in 1908. She is a very handsome schooner and, like most of these big East coast-built vessels, she has a very powerful and graceful sheer. Because of their length, most of these later schooners 'hogged', that is dropped at the ends and tended to lose their sheer quite early in their lives. As the later photographs show, the *Bertha L Downs* was still as handsome when she was 30 years old. She is launched complete and ready for sea. Even the gaff topsails can be seen neatly furled at the lowermast heads. (Bath Marine Museum)

93 The *Bertha L Downs* in her days with the Benedict Manson Marine Company and bearing the name of the port of Newhaven, Connecticut, on her stern. She is deep laden and almost becalmed. When he saw this photograph, Captain Karl V Karlsson commented that her fore, main and mizzen gaff topsails should be taken in, unless an immediate change of weather was expected, since, flapping about as they are against the triatic or jump stays, they would be damaged before long. (W J Lewis Parker)

94 LEFT One of the masters of the *Bertha L Downs* under the United States flag was Captain Stinson F Davis, shown here, right, relaxing with his brother Irving Davis when both were serving in the schooner *Maria O Teel* which was commanded by a third brother, Captain Will Davis. Captain Stinson Davis celebrated his 93rd birthday at his home in Five Islands, Maine, in 1978, while this book was being written. (W J Lewis Parker)

95 In 1917 the *Bertha L Downs* was sold to Danish owners, renamed *Atlas* and employed in the Baltic timber trade to Western Europe. This photograph, below, shows her lying in the River Thames under the Danish flag with an enormous deck cargo of timber built up even the greater part of the length of her poop deck. (National Maritime Museum)

96 Lumber cargoes like that shown in the last photograph were loaded at Swedish ports on the west coast of the Gulf of Bothnia. The *Atlas* lay out in the roadsteads at anchor and the lumber was brought alongside in barges and stowed by gangs of women stevedores called 'splitvedjäntor', which could be translated 'lathwood lassies'. The timber was the offcuts of the local sawmills, from 18 inches to 6 feet long, boards and battens, mostly pine, used in Britain and western Europe for a number of different purposes, such as furniture-making, the making of fruit boxes, fish boxes and crates, for fencing, for the paving of roads in the days of horses, and the small damaged stuff for firewood. It was loaded into the *Atlas* with the old oil engine working the cargo gaffs seen rigged in this photograph, below. Up to 40 women handled the cargo, many of them, from surviving photographs, young and pretty, and they were very quick to sort out the material which had been thrown higgledy-piggledy into the barges and to stow it both in the hold and in the deck cargo, though it was killing work. The crew worked the winches and cargo gaffs, but they never touched the lumber. (Ålands Sjöfarts-museum)

97 The timber which came to London was discharged mainly in the Surrey Commercial Docks and the Regents Canal Dock. In this photograph, right, the *Atlas* is seen in the Regents Canal Dock during the years she sailed from the Åland Islands. She is discharging a part of her cargo which comprises short lengths of timber into a lighter. (Ålands Sjöfartsmuseum)

98 I saw the *Atlas* lying in Copenhagen in the 1930s, discharging a cargo of timber from the Gulf of Bothnia, and was immensely impressed by the fact that she had retained her very powerful sheer, although she was 30 years old, and by the grace and strength of her hull. Perhaps that was another occasion when this book began. This photograph shows her lying there with five members of her crew perched on the bowsprit and jibboom – note that she retained a full jibboom with martingale throughout her long working life and note also the strength of her bows. (Basil Greenhill)

99 When she was owned in the Åland Islands, Captain Karl V Karlsson was Master of the *Atlas*. I took this photograph of him in retirement outside his home in Vårdö in 1977. Captain Karlsson spent many years in wooden sailing ships and also commanded the steel four-masted barque *Parma* in the Australian grain trade round Cape Horn. While this book was being written in 1978 he celebrated his eightieth birthday. The long-lived *Atlas* seems to have shared her qualities with her masters. (Basil Greenhill)

100 The *Prindsesse Alice*, ex *Atlas*, ex *Bertha L Downs*, photographed on 27 June 1948, being broken up at Kiel at the end of her long working life. Many of the big American schooners were comparatively short-lived. The 40 years of this very fine vessel were exceptional. (Dr Jürgen Meyer)

Some Schooners of the World

The schooner rig was used in various forms all over the world. Several of the different types of local schooners which existed in the early years of this century probably represented separate developments of the schooner from different sources – the sail plan comprising two or more fore and aft sails with the greater part of the canvas aft was a natural one and, as we have already seen, could develop by different routes from different origins.

In this section of this book are photographs showing local schooners in six different parts of the world – the Baltic, a steel schooner from Denmark, France, Greece, Syria and New Zealand. Each vessel has strongly marked local characteristics. Two of them, the Finnish galeas and the Syrian schooner, probably developed quite independently of the main stream of the evolution of the schooner in Europe and North America.

Two of the photographs show European four-masted schooners. During the shipbuilding boom generated by the First World War, some 14 small four-masters were built of wood in Denmark, some of them with square topsails on the the foremast, besides one or two of steel. About the same number were built of wood in Finland and some of steel after the war in Germany and Holland. Perhaps the last to be built was the auxiliary *Ida IV* launched at Westerbrook, Holland, in 1927 and in due course sold to South American owners.

101 The skonertskepp *Svea*, launched at Finström in Åland
in 1920, represents another type of Baltic merchant
schooner, the big three-master with square yards on her
foretopmast, that is the skonertskepp as opposed to the
slättoppare, the schooner without yards. Notice that she has
a brailing foresail like a galeas. She is here shown with a big
cargo of timber including a high deck cargo on which a
member of the crew is standing mid-way between the fore
and main masts. The *Svea*, built in the World War One
shipping boom but launched too late to make much money
from it, like most of the wooden sailing vessels built at that
period was cheaply constructed. She began leaking heavily
in 1931 and during 1931, 1932 and 1933 she swung to her
anchor in the Bay of Båthusvik in Vårdö in Åland. In 1934
she was sold for use as a steamer jetty in the Parish of
Kumlinge in the outer skerries of the Åland Islands. (Ålands
Sjöfartsmuseum)

102 The galeas *Augusta* of Kallvik. The galeas of the Finnish and Swedish archipelagoes was a local type of schooner which evolved very rapidly in the nineteenth century from a two-masted vessel with squaresails on each mast, the main – the taller of the two – being in the fore part of the vessel – a kind of square-rigged ketch. The vessels were undecked and clinker-built. In about 50 years gaff sails replaced the squaresails and the open clinker-built hulls were replaced by skeleton-built decked vessels. In due course the masts were developed to be of the same height.

Apart from the crossing of the Åland Sea between the two archipelagoes, for which the time and weather could usually be carefully chosen, these vessels operated usually in sheltered waters with hundreds of available sheltering places on their trade routes among the skerries and they did not sail in the depth of winter when the sea was frozen. They often operated in the very narrow waterways lined with tall trees. In these circumstances a sail plan was developed to fit the local conditions, with very tall masts, especially tall topmasts, long narrow square-headed gaff topsails and big long-luffed lower sails which brailed into the masts on rings which slid along boom and gaff so that the gaffs were never lowered. The term galeas became locally associated with this schooner sail plan, so that in the present century a three-masted schooner without square topsails was sometimes referred to, and even legally registered as, a three-masted galeas. Even the four-masted barquentine *Dione* designed as a 'slättoppare', a schooner without square topsails on her foremast, and built as late as 1921, was referred to in her early documentation as a four-masted galeas.

The *Augusta* herself was built at Nagu in Finland as the *Juni* (June) in 1875. After about ten years she was sold to A A Soderholm at Ostra Ed Kalmar in Sweden, and she remained owned in the Kalmar district, latterly by Johan Fritz Andersson at Kallvik. She was hulked about 1930 and her remains could still be seen in the late 1960s.

The *Augusta* is carrying a deck cargo of small timber in the photograph. This is firewood, probably destined for Stockholm. The trade in firewood from the Finnish archipelago and latterly from the coast of mainland Finland across the Gulf of Bothnia to Stockholm was one of the principal occupations of these galeaser, the last of which were still working in the 1930s. Some survive today in altered forms as yachts and cruise vessels. (National Maritime Museum)

103 This is the crew of the skonertskepp *Nils* owned by Leander Olofsson of the parish of Vårdö in the Åland Islands and built in 1879. The photograph illustrates very well the after accommodation, a deck house surrounded by a low poop deck, of one of these big Baltic three-masted schooners.

The master, seated second from the left, is K Karlsson; fourth from the left is the mate, Mr Palmqvist and seated next to him is Cook Okand. Åland schooners often carried women cooks. (Ålands Sjöfartsmuseum)

104 This photograph is deliberately included to confuse, and to show that it is unwise to attempt to impose too much rigidity on the definitions of the rigs of sailing ships.

Indeed, the definitions used in this book are essentially British/American of the late nineteenth century, and simplified at that. There were very many variations in the world and in history. This photograph shows one of them: she is the *Balder*, built in the parish of Lemland in the Åland Islands in 1922 and shown with a big deck cargo of Baltic timber. She has a fully square-rigged foremast and in British eyes is a barquentine, but besides the square foresail she also gets from her fore lowermast a gaff and boom sail as big as her mizzen. Vessels of this type, together with three-masted schooners with squaresails on the fore topmasts like the *Svea* in Plate 102 and ordinary barquentines are all lumped together in the Swedish language used in the Åland Islands as 'skonertskepp' – literally 'schooner ship' – an excellent way of describing vessels with such combinations of square and gaff rig. The Swedes and Finns in developing their terminology were not forced into somewhat artificial particularisation, as were the British, and to some extent the Americans, by the administration of merchant shipping legislation. (Ålands Sjöfartsmuseum)

105 The very handsome four-masted schooner *Yxpila* has all the appearance of a West coast United States-built vessel (see Plates 79 and 80), but in fact she was built on the mainland of Finland in 1920, one of four very similar vessels constructed by a Finnish master shipwright who had lived in the United States and worked in West coast shipyards. She is shown entering Dover harbour under tow, laden with a timber cargo.

Yxpila was a very handy and successful vessel, although like most of the wooden sailing ships built in the shipbuilding boom of the First World War, she was cheaply constructed. Nevertheless she lasted for many years. She was handy and fast and, as has already been said in the second section of this book, she was a pleasure to sail.

Yxpila was laid up in Åbo in 1948 and driven aground in a storm on the night of 25 October that year. She was refloated but never again went to sea, finally sinking at her anchors in 1952. (National Maritime Museum)

106 By way of contrast, a year before the *Yxpila* was built of timber from the forests of Finland, the four-masted schooner *Margot* was launched at Svendborg in Denmark, a copy of a small American four-master in steel, also with the intention of profiting from the shipping boom which followed the First World War. She was probably in time to benefit at least from the last year or two of it.

In 1921 she was sold to Swedish owners and it was during this period of her life that this photograph was taken while she was discharging cargo at Littlehampton in England. In 1926 she was sold again to owners in Auckland, New Zealand, although for some reason she was registered as of the Port of London, England. She was renamed *Margaret W*, she was employed in trade across the Tasman Sea and on the New Zealand coast. In 1929 she was sold to the Gisborne Sheep-Farmers Frozen Meat and Mercantile Co Ltd and traded consistently between Gisborne and Auckland with general cargo and produce. She was broken up in 1957 in Hong Kong after sailing under the Chilean flag. (National Maritime Museum)

107 In the second half of the last century and the first 35 years of this one a big fleet of two- and three-masted schooners sailed from ports in Brittany. In the present century many of these vessels were employed in carrying cargoes of timber for pit props from small ports in Brittany to Cardiff and as late as 1937 there were still 15 of them employed in this trade along with the same number of ketches. A characteristic of these Breton schooners was the big square foretopsail which was reefed and furled by an ingenious roller device. This was very handy and efficient and saved the necessity of working aloft until the sail itself was furled and had to be made fast. Used in only three British schooners (in which it was very successful) the gear was probably not adopted in Britain generally because the rather complicated ironwork for it was not readily available. The schooner La Mouette of Tréguier is approaching the entrance to the harbour at Penzance in Cornwall and this photograph illustrates the big square topsail set from a roller clearly visible below the foretopsail yard. (The late H Oliver Hill)

108 The roller reefing topsail in the process of being taken in. Simply by pulling furling lines on the deck it has literally been rolled up on the spar to which it is secured, which is beneath the fore topsail yard and slung from it on iron brackets and claws. A man is aloft to check that the reefing gear is working and clear anything which fouls. He is standing on the lower masthead and holding the fore topmast.

Note that this vessel is also equipped with a brailing foresail which is now being taken in, the gaff being left standing aloft. The combination of the roller reefing topsail and the brailing foresail made for saving of manpower and for ease and simplicity in handling the vessel, which is *La Revanche Hennebont* of Lorient, photographed off Newlyn on 20 March, 1926 by the great pioneer contemporary recorder of the last merchant schooners and working boats. (The late H Oliver Hill)

109 The Syrian schooner was a well-developed local type of vessel built on the Syrian and Lebanese coasts and in Egypt. Latterly, that is in the 1940s, building was apparently confined to the Island of Ruad off Tartus in Syria and the vessels were engaged in seasonal trade to Egypt.

The Syrian schooner had many features of interest. The most obvious was her rig. She was one of the very few merchant vessel types in the world to use the shoulder-of-mutton, the jib-headed, so-called Bermudan, triangular sail universal in modern yachts, though her sails with their low aspect ratio were of a very different form from those used by yachtsmen in the late twentieth century.

Almost certainly the origin of the rig here, as in North America where it also developed independently on Chesapeake Bay, was with a lateen sail, the yard more and more steeply canted until the yard itself was stepped and became the mast.

Notice the side cloths rigged to keep spray from the deck cargo. The use of side cloth was widespread on sailing vessels in the eastern Mediterranean.

Schooners of the type shown in this illustration were still being built at Ruad in 1949. I saw no less than eleven of them lying in the Sound between Ruad and the mainland in February 1954, and a number of others in Egyptian waters four years later. (C L Barker)

110 The most common type of rig on small vessels trading among the Greek Islands and around the little harbours of the mainland was that of two balanced lug sails, or one balanced lug and one standing lug, set from pole masts of much the same height. But in the twentieth century many of these small ships were converted into small schooners by the simple process of replacing the lug sails with their yards with gaff and boom sails on the existing masts in the existing positions. The result was a characteristic type of small pole-masted schooner and on a long journey through Greece in 1954 I saw several hundred such vessels of varying sizes. This photograph shows one of them becalmed in the Gulf of Corinth. Notice her big deck cargo and the side cloths used, as in the Syrian schooner, to protect it. (Basil Greenhill)

111 The New Zealand scow schooner *Lady St Clair* is on the right. The New Zealand scow, originally locally called a schooner barge, was a most interesting local variation, not of the schooner rig, for she was equipped with the normal spars and sails of a two or three-masted schooner, but of the use of the rig on a very shallow draught, flat-bottomed hull.

The scow hull form was almost certainly brought to New Zealand by settlers from the eastern parts of Canada and the United States, where such hull forms were common. She was in fact a huge punt, which after a few years of building them was refined by the addition of a stem and sharp bows. But the great majority of scows always carried all their cargo on deck and depended on drop keels for any ability to sail to windward.

The scow was a product of a requirement for economical operation both in very shallow tidal creeks and rivers where timber was loaded from waterside mills and on the stormy coasts of New Zealand. Some even sailed across the Tasman Sea to Australia.

The first scow, the *Southern Cross*, was built in 1873. The vessel shown on the right here, the *Lady St Clair* in her old age, was built in 1876. The scow in the background, which has not been identified, shows the simple American-style two-masted schooner rig adopted in most of these vessels. (National Maritime Museum)

The Last Days of the Schooners

The only real index to the growth and decline of different types of ships, wooden square-rigged sailing vessels, iron screw steamers with compound engines, steel screw steamers with triple expansion engines, the big wooden schooners and the iron and steel square-rigged sailing vessels which developed at about the same time, is the rate of new construction. On this basis the wooden square-rigged ship was obsolete by the middle 1870s, the big iron and steel square-rigged sailing ship by the end of the century after a life of only 25 years, and the big wooden schooner about 7 years later. But then the big schooner enjoyed a short new life which the square-rigged vessel never had as a result of the building boom all over the world during and after the First World War.

The small schooner, carrying up to 250 tons of cargo and often much less, survived much longer. Although the last to be built in the United Kingdom was launched in 1913, they continued to be launched in, among other places, Newfoundland, Spain and Denmark until well into the 1940s and Nova Scotian and Danish schooners traded regularly across the Atlantic in the Newfoundland trade until the Second World War.

At the outbreak of that war there were still one hundred schooners and ketches fitted with auxiliary motors and three sailing schooners without motors trading on the coasts of Britain besides a number of trading smacks. Of these nearly half, nine three-masted schooners and 32 ketches, were owned in Appledore in North Devon or in Braunton a mile or two away on the other side of the estuary of the Torridge. Except for a few steel vessels bought from Holland after the First World War and the wooden ketch *Dido C* (Plates 51 and 121) they were all old, or very old, vessels. Some of them dated from the 1860s.

Schooners and ketches by the hundred were still trading among the Danish Islands and in Greek and Turkish waters in the mid-1950s. At the same time the remains of an only recently disbanded great fleet could still be seen at Viareggio on the west coast of Italy. Schooners lasted even longer in trade in the West Indies. Indeed the small schooner fitted with an auxiliary engine eventually succumbed less to the competition of the fully powered vessel than to that of motor transport on land, which destroyed the coasting trades of many countries, to the rising cost of labour and to new methods of packaging and handling goods, and to the development of industry and trade beyond the point at which there was any demand to carry small cargoes on deep water.

If continued new construction, development of design, and the operation in large numbers of vessels using sails to assist their diesel engines are the indicators, then the last merchant sailing ship-owning nation in the western world was Denmark. In 1950 there were still nearly one thousand vessels owned in Denmark (including the Faroe Islands) which were fitted with masts and sails. Of the 592 vessels legally registered at ports in metropolitan Denmark about 85 were schooners and the rest ketches and trading smacks – galeaser, as they were known, in opposition to the use of the term in the Åland Islands, where it meant two-masted schooners, and jagter. Many of the larger ketches and schooners were trading across the North Sea, to Iceland and, even as late as 1949, to Greenland. At least 20 big wooden schooners and ketches were built after 1940 and some of these vessels incorporated developments in hull form and rigging which carried the small merchant auxiliary sailing vessel to her final stage.

The construction of bridges between many adjacent islands, the development of roads and of big, regularly running, roll-on roll-off ferries, the rising cost of labour – this was most important of all – and the rising costs of sails and rigging all worked together to eliminate this great fleet in the 1960s. Today none is left working with sails, though some are used as yachts and charter vessels. They can be seen lying in a number of Danish harbours and they provide a close parallel with the London River sailing barges which passed out of commercial use at about the same time and can now be seen in lines in St Katharine's Dock, London, and at Maldon, Essex and elsewhere.

In different parts of the world, a few vessels of different kinds have been preserved, sometimes much altered from their appearance when working. They include the schooner *Kathleen & May* and the ketches *Shamrock* and *Garlandstone* in Britain, the three-masted *Result* in northern Ireland, the fishing schooners *L A Dunton* at Mystic, Connecticut, *Teresa Connor* at Lunenberg, Nova Scotia and *Norma & Gladys* at St John's, Newfoundland. On the west coast of North America the three-masters *Wawona* and *C A Thayer* serve as museum ships, while in Norwegian waters the Danish-built *Svanen* has been preserved in seagoing condition, though much changed from her days as a working vessel. Some Danish schooners and ketches now used as yachts are little changed from their appearance as merchant vessels. Perhaps the finest preserved schooner in the world is Danish, the old Marstal Newfoundland trader *Fulton*, lovingly and scrupulously reconstructed as she was in her great days in the North Atlantic trade and still sailing among the Danish islands with crews of young people.

112 The great *Cora F Cressy* (see Plate 71) lies today a huge, rotting, wooden hulk in a creek at Bremen, Maine; a small tree grows out of her bowsprit and some of her fittings have been moved to the Marine Museum at Bath, Maine, where they are on display at the Percy and Small shipyard site, but age has not concealed the power of her huge bows. This photograph of the great hulk was taken in the spring of 1978. (Basil Greenhill)

113 The same fate overtook many of the later big American schooners. Here are two four-masters, slowly reverting to nature, at Wiscasset in Maine. Both were built at Somerset, Massachusetts, during the First World War building boom. The *Hesper*, the vessel in the background in this photograph, was early enough to profit her builders, making trans-Atlantic passages and voyages to South America.

The *Luther Little* of 1917 was also in time to make money on deep water. At the time of writing in early 1979 she still has her four masts in her and, although in a very derelict condition, is the last rigged survivor of all the hundreds of four-masted wooden schooners built in the world between 1879 and the early 1920s. (Basil Greenhill)

114 Old merchant schooners have been put to new uses. From Camden, Rockport, Rockland, Belfast and some other places on the Maine coast, as well as on the coast of Massachusetts and in the West Indies, old merchant schooners have been brought back to life, sometimes from a state of advanced dereliction, partly rebuilt, and refitted as cruise vessels. On the Maine coast it is possible, with hard work and enthusiasm and a good deal of expertise, to make a reasonable living operating a vessel of this kind under sail alone in the summer months in suitable waters.

Here are two of the Maine cruise schooners, both old merchant vessels, the *Mattie* ex *Grace Baily*, built at Patchogue, New York State in 1882, and the *Mercantile* built at Deer Isle, Maine, in 1916. Both now operate from Camden, Maine, and were photographed there in 1978. They had been prepared for their winter lay-up and fitted with plastic covers to protect their decks and fittings from the snow and frost and freezing rain. (Basil Greenhill)

115 The old west coast lumber schooner *C A Thayer* is shown, right, under repair in San Francisco where she is preserved. She has pole masts, that is masts without separate fidded topmasts. Pole masts were characteristic of many of these West coast vessels. *C A Thayer* was built at Fairhaven in 1895. (Dr John H Harland)

116 This is the *Lois M Candage*, built at Bluehill, Maine in 1912, and photographed at Damariscotta, Maine, in 1969. A typical small Maine two-master, built to trade in the local waters to the islands and around the coast, like so many other vessels of her type all over the world she was eventually abandoned and left to fall to pieces where she lay. (Basil Greenhill)

117 The *Margaret Hobley* was built at Pembroke, West Wales, in 1868 and remained in trade until the Second World War, latterly owned by the Slade family of Appledore, the last owners of a fleet of schooners in Britain. Shown here off the South Wales coast, for most of her long life she was a three-masted schooner with square topsails on her fore topmast. This photograph illustrates what happened to most British schooners sooner or later after the First World War. She has been fitted with a powerful auxiliary engine, her topmasts have been reduced to short sticks and her mizzenmast shortened. In this particular case her masts have been re-stepped to bring her foremast aft and take some of the weight out of her bows and her lower sails have been much reduced in size. She has been fitted with tiny gaff topsails bought from some other much smaller vessel. She still carried enough canvas for it to be possible to sail her, but her principal means of propulsion was her diesel engine. (National Maritime Museum)

140

118 LEFT The three-masted motor schooner *Haldon* at anchor off Dover. Owned and commanded by Captain W J Slade, the author of the classic autobiography *Out of Appledore*, she was one of the most successful of the latter day British motor schooners. She was built at Plymouth in 1893 as a ketch and when she was adapted as an auxiliary motor vessel in the 1920s Captain Slade decided to make her into a three-masted schooner to reduce the size of the individual sails and the wear and tear and cost of maintenance. The reduction in sail area was done very thoughtfully and the vessel as shown in the photograph, with her pole masts and simple rigging, represents an efficient, and at the time profitable, combination of power and sail. (National Maritime Museum)

119 One of the last merchant schooners in British waters to sail without an auxiliary engine and perhaps the last to survive (albeit laid up) without one, was the *Mary Stewart* of Ardrossan built at Ardrossan in 1868. For years after her last voyage (before the Second World War) she was laid up in the harbour at Scarinish on the Isle of Tiree and she was still there in the second half of the 1940s.
This photograph shows her hull still intact dried out at low water in the tidal harbour. (Basil Greenhill Collection)

120 RIGHT The schooner *Helena Anna* was built in 1870. This photograph, which I took in 1937, typifies the fate of a great many wooden schooners the world over. Not profitable to break up, they were left to fall to pieces in quiet backwaters of the creeks and rivers of Maine, Prince Edward Island and Nova Scotia, in the sounds between the Danish islands, in the *viks* of the Åland Islands, on mud banks in corners of San Francisco Harbour and at the back of St Malo, and, in this case, in Pont Pill off Fowey Harbour in Cornwall.
Vessels like this, slowly dying in a quiet backwater after years of sailing, often over half the world, had about them an atmosphere difficult to describe, powerfully redolent of past human endeavour. (Basil Greenhill)

121 On the morning of 16 September 1936, the crew of the ketch *Dido C* ex *Jules Claes* (see Plate 51) made an error of judgement of a type most unusual among seamen so familiar with the tides, rocks and mudbanks of the Bristol Channel where they were constantly sailing. Cutting inside the outer reefs of the wild coast of North Devon in hazy weather, they grounded on one of the ledges off Morte Point. As the tide ebbed the vessel was in such a dangerous position that the crew were taken off by the Ilfracombe lifeboat *Rosabella*, but as the flood tide rose the crew were put on board again and in the same afternoon the *Dido C* was towed off. She continued working for another ten years after this remarkable photograph was taken and her escape from very serious damage can be attributed to four factors. She had no cargo, the weight of which would have strained her beyond repair. Had she been an old or a poorly built vessel she would have been ruined even though she had no cargo but, only 15 years old, she was much the youngest wooden auxiliary sailing vessel on the British coast – and she had been specially and expensively built as an engine demonstration ship. Finally the sea remained smooth so that she was not pounded on the rocks as the tide fell and rose. (Knights Photographers)

122 The *Rhoda Mary* in her last days. The schooner *Rhoda Mary* built near Devoran within the port area of Truro in 1868, was one of the two or three finest, fastest and most famous merchant schooners ever built in Britain. She traded to the Mediterranean, the Baltic and to the Gulf of Finland and for years in the home trade around the British coasts. For twenty years 61 of the shares in her were owned by a syndicate of Warders in Dartmoor Gaol, the remaining three by her Master, Samson Westlake of Gunnislake in Cornwall. This photograph, taken in 1947, shows her abandoned in her old age and like the *Helena Anna*, slowly falling to pieces, this time in the Medway opposite Gillingham. (Basil Greenhill)

123 The small ketch *Shamrock* was built by Frederick Hawke at Stonehouse, Plymouth, England in 1899 for the local trade of the rivers Tamar, Plym, and Lynher and on the adjacent coasts as far as Falmouth, trades comparable with those in which the *Lois M Candage* (Plate 116) was employed on the other side of the Atlantic. Between 1975 and 1979 she was completely rebuilt and refitted at Cotehele Quay in Cornwall under the supervision of Tom Perkins and the National Maritime Museum to her appearance and outfit as in 1926, when this photograph was taken. She now lies in the tidal dock there, adjacent to the National Maritime Museum's outpost gallery of the maritime industrial history of the region, as the gallery's biggest exhibit. Owned by the National Trust and the National Maritime Museum, she is one of the most carefully and thoroughly restored small wooden merchant sailing vessels in the world. (National Maritime Museum)

124 The three-masted schooner *Kathleen & May* was built at Connah's Quay in Clwyd, North Wales, in 1900. She spent the whole of her life in the home trade, being fitted with an auxiliary engine in the early 1920s and with successively more powerful engines in the next thirty years, although she retained pole masts and a good spread of canvas and could always be handled as a sailing vessel. She made her last passage with cargo in 1960 and is now preserved by the Maritime Trust in St Katharine's Dock in London, restored more or less to her appearance as a schooner with square topsails on her foremast.

I took this photograph off the Welsh coast in September, 1959, when the vessel was on passage from Bristol towards Milford Haven with feeding stuffs. (Basil Greenhill)

125 The *Kathleen & May* takes a short run down hill. The vessel is rolling and pitching heavily in a big ground sea, proceeding under power and sail in a very light breeze. (Basil Greenhill)

126 The wheelhouse of the *Freyapaket* built at Svendborg in 1923 by J Ring-Anderson, one of the most famous Danish schooner builders. The wheelhouse was added with her auxiliary engine in 1944. Listed on her name board are the ports between which, even in the second half of the twentieth century, she maintained a regular service, like a packet boat in Britain before the development of the railways or a country carrier's cart before motor trucks. The poor *Freyapaket* ended her career far from the idyllic South Danish Islands as a film ship under the name of *Hispaniola*. She was lost in the Bay of Biscay. (Basil Greenhill)

127 Before the building of bridges, the establishment of regular roll-on roll-off ferries, and general changes in the economy of the country in the second half of the twentieth century, a great part of the trade between the various islands of Denmark was carried on in particularly efficient and often handsome small motor schooners, and galeaser (ketches). These were the last merchant auxiliary sailing vessels to exist in any numbers in the western world. Here is the *Jens Juhl* built at Nykøbing in 1940. She is discharging a tractor from a deck cargo at Svendborg in 1949. The cargo included, besides Ferguson tractors, hides, carboys of acid, crates of Rinso, a four-wheeled trailer, mixed groceries in packages, oil in drums, and lengths of pipe. (Basil Greenhill)

128 RIGHT The transom stern of the *Jens Juhl*, although she was built at Nykøbing was characteristic of Marstal on the Island of Aerø, a great Newfoundland trade port which closely paralleled Porthmadog in North Wales in its ship-owning and seafaring activities. The stern shape, which was efficient and economical, was copied also in Sweden – see the stern of the Swedish-built *Jules Claes* later *Dido C* in Plate 51. (Basil Greenhill)

129 A Danish motor galease setting the same sort of reduced sails as the *Jens Juhl* used at the time the photographs of her were taken. This photograph was taken soon after the Second World War and shows the vessel with wartime markings. The *Bien* (bee) was built at Marstal in 1898 and owned when the photograph was taken by O V Jørgensen at Fjellebroen. (Basil Greenhill)

130 Latter day Danish motor schooners and galeaser could be found setting any amount of canvas from the minimum necessary for them to be sailed, like the *Bien*, to the full sails set by a vessel before diesel engines were thought of. Here is the *Havet*, built at Svendborg in 1939 by J Ring-Anderson and owned there. In 1950 she still looked as she does in this photograph and she was spoken of in Denmark as the finest surviving galease. (Basil Greenhill Collection)

131 Similarly the *slettop-skonnert* (schooner without square yards on her fore topmast) *Annette S* was built as late as 1944, yet she has the full spar and sail plan of a schooner of the early 1900s. Her topsails are even stowed aloft, instead of being set from the deck of jackstays. Notice the beautiful elliptical counter stern, characteristic of Svendborg where she was built by the great J Ring-Anderson. I took this photograph in 1949 in Svendborg Sound when the vessel was about to set sail on a voyage across the Atlantic to load cargo in Greenland. The *slettop-skonnert* ('slättoppare' in Swedish), so like the Canadian tern schooner, became very common in Denmark, Sweden and Finland in the 20th century. She was a late development of the European schooner. The first in Denmark, the *Meta*, was built in 1903, but similar vessels were built in mainland Finland in the early 1890s and registered as three masted galeaser. It seems likely that the 'slättopare' represents a separate development of the three masted schooner from the Finnish galeas, the vessels illustrated in Plates 8 and 102.

132 This photograph, taken in Copenhagen in 1949, shows the complete contrast between a classic British small schooner hull form and the highly developed shape of the last merchant schooners to be built in Europe.
The vessel on the left is the *Bjørn Olafsson* of Copenhagen built as the *Clulov* at Bideford, England by H M Restarick in 1884 and employed when this photograph was taken in the Danish coasting trade. The vessel on the right with her cruiser stern and with three pole masts all the same height is the *Hans Albert*, a three-masted wooden motor schooner built at Holbaek in 1944, one of the last merchant schooners built in northern Europe. (Basil Greenhill)

133 Here is Jørgen Ring-Anderson himself, the last great European schooner builder, photographed by the author in his yard at Svendborg in 1949. The Ring-Anderson yard is still in business and in recent years refitted the *Anna Møller* (Plate 137) for the Danish National Museum. Jørgen Ring-Anderson built over 100 ships, his father built 80. The last sailing merchant vessel he built was the galease *Ring-Anderson* of 1948. (Basil Greenhill)

134 The three-masted slettop-skonnert *Fulton* was built at Marstal by C L Johansen in 1915 and in her early days was employed principally in the Newfoundland stockfish trade between Denmark, Newfoundland, the Mediterranean and Britain. Reduced in later life to a two-masted motor ship she has been completely restored by the Danish National Museum to her appearance as a merchant sailing vessel. She sails in summer with a permanent crew and groups of young people. This photograph was taken in The Sound in 1970 when the *Fulton* met the Danish full-rigged ship training vessel *Danmark* on her way back to Copenhagen from a long deep water voyage. (Basil Greenhill)

135 This photograph shows the young people setting the foresail in the *Fulton*. The job is not being done perfectly. The gaff should be kept parallel with the boom until the luff of the sail (usually referred to by the crews of British schooners as the 'weather' of the sail) is taut and the gaff then peaked up with the peak halyards, the two blocks of which are clearly visible towards the end of the gaff. The *Fulton* is a lovely vessel, sailed well and properly maintained. (Basil Greenhill)

136 The *Fulton* setting sail. Notice her Marstal type transom stern. The master stands on the stern rail while the permanent crew supervise the young people at the work. Because the young people spend only a week or so on board only maintenance work is done aloft and the gaff topsails are set on wire jackstays from on deck. (Basil Greenhill)

137 The Danish National Museum has also restored and refitted the galease *Anna Møller* which now lies afloat in the middle of Copenhagen in Nyhaven where I took this photograph in June 1978. She is about the same size as the *Shamrock* (Plate 123) and rigged similarly but is a rather grander vessel. Like the *Shamrock* she has been meticulously restored under museum supervision to her appearance and outfit as a merchant vessel. She was built as the *Esther* at Randers in 1906. (Basil Greenhill)

138 Here is another survivor, the *Svanen*, built at Svendborg by Ring-Anderson in 1920 and now owned in Norway as a sailing museum ship. She was photographed in the mouth of the Oslo fjord one rain-swept windy day in 1975.

She has been much altered from her form as a merchant vessel. Notice the small booms set very high to clear the deckhouses which have been built on her, the davits from which a plastic motor boat is slung, and the nylon sails. (Basil Greenhill)

139 TOP This unknown goelette of the St Lawrence with her high deck cargo of small timber illustrates the simple schooners which developed to carry the extensive local trade on the tidewater of this huge river, its estuary, and the adjacent waterways.

The goelettes bore a remarkable resemblance in hull form to the cogs of medieval northern Europe. Like the cogs they were flat-bottomed, with rounded sides and sloping straight stem and stern posts. In fact their general form was like that of a gigantic Swampscott dory.

The goelette is illustrated here, rather than in the last section of this book, because she was a survivor. Though this photograph was taken on the St Lawrence in 1906, many of them were still in trade as auxiliary motor vessels in the 1930s and 1940s. (National Maritime Museum)

140 ABOVE From the sailing goelette developed the fully powered goelette, but not until well into the twentieth century. She had the schooner's basic hull form, flat-bottomed and straight stemmed, but with a motorship's superstructure and latterly no masts and sails, but she kept the name of goelette. The last of these vessels to be built, and probably the last sizeable wooden merchant ship ever to be built in the western world, was the *Jean Richard*, launched at Petite-Rivière-St-François on the north shore of the St Lawrence in Quebec Province in 1959. This photograph, showing her as she is today after conversion into a passenger vessel under the name *Ville de Vanier*. was taken at Hull in Quebec in the autumn of 1978. (Basil Greenhill)

141 The schooner, that is working schooner hulls motor driven but still retaining some vestiges of masts, rigging and sails and still employed commercially, ended where she really began – on the north-east coast of the North American continent. Here is one of the very last of them – the *Mary Ruth*, built at Shelburne, Nova Scotia in 1918 as a fully-rigged, two-masted schooner for the dory fishery for cod on the North Atlantic banks, registered at La Have, Nova Scotia and owned in Lunenberg, photographed as she lay dishevelled and run-down but still at work at Brigus, Newfoundland in March 1977, the long raking counter cut off her stern, her masts reduced, her bowsprit long gone, a high deckhouse built on and an electric pump endlessly lifting over her side the clear water which poured in through her aged seams. The *Mary Ruth* was one of the last real, unrestored, relics of a world we have now completely lost. (Basil Greenhill)